COMMUNICATING READERS THEATRE

Messages in Group Performance

Todd V. Lewis

Biola University

KENDALL/HUNT PUBLISHING COMPANY
4050 Westmark Drive   Dubuque, Iowa 52002

Dedicated to my grandsons,
Harrison Lewis Price and Jackson Lee Price

Cover image courtesy of Stockdisc/Getty Images, licensed by Biola University

Cover and book design by Jonathan Price

Printed in the United States of America
10 9 8 7 6 5 4 3 2 1

Contents

i

Chapter 3 Transforming Texts into Group Performance: Selection and Analysis

Chapter 4 Performance Choices

Chapter 5   **Adapting Texts:**
Drama/Narrative Fiction/Poetry

Chapter 6   **Adapting Texts:**
Nonfiction Prose/Ethnographies/"Oral" Texts

Chapter 7   Designing and Staging the Textual Performance

Chapter 8   Creativity in Textual Performances

Chapter 9   Preparing the Production Guide/Script; Rehearsals in Preparation for Performance

Chapter 10 Outlets for Readers Theatre Performance

Preface

I remember it vividly as though it were yesterday rather than more than thirty-five years ago. I had completed an undergraduate course in oral interpretation as part of my degree work at Biola University, but it was not until I reached graduate school at Ohio State University in the early 1970s that I was introduced to "Readers Theatre." I signed up for a course that doubled as a senior undergraduate/first year graduate student course in "Readers Theatre," and in addition to creating a production guide for a possible public presentation I was asked to join others in the class as a performer of literature. I thought I was able to reasonably offer up the "husband" role in the free-verse poem, "Home Burial" by Robert Frost, but my performing skills were taxed beyond my limit so I thought, when the professor assigned me to the role of the black South African minister in Alan Paton's anti-apartheid 1948 novel excerpt, *Cry, the Beloved Country*. I understood that oral interpretation and readers theatre theory asked me to "suggest" rather than "actualize" my character, but I was not black, not South African, not a minister—and I was befuddled with what I would do in performance. I thought my choices were constricted, certainly not very deep or revealing of commitment, but I learned something in this difficult assignment. The "text" was so powerful and compelling that despite my own perceived limitations the audience reactions revealed an emotional response to the inherent message of this text. I seem to remember getting a "B" on the performance—which I thought was generous at the time. But even though I could not "represent" in a real fashion the main character of this novel, something happened with our group performance that resonated with the audience. We must have found the "essence" of the message of this text and the "suggestion" in performance was enough to make the point.

Readers Theatre and all presentational group performance attempts have the capacity to bring all kinds of literature and printed and spoken "texts" to an arena for consideration of intent and message. This textbook will attempt to give you a means to discover how to adapt a wide variety of performance texts for audiences of all ages and perspectives. You should discover, as I did, that you do not need to "actualize" a character that is unlike you, but you will find ways to bring your own experiences and associations into performance "choices" that hopefully focus on the apparent intent of the text. Readers Theatre is not dry and static group reading, without rehearsal or consideration of performance choices or exploration of character or text. It is a dynamic different "theatrical" experience that brings to a performance "space" an opportunity for audiences to primarily "imagine" what is being offered.

This textbook is intended for students in an advanced oral interpretation/performance studies course or a course labeled as "Readers Theatre" or "Interpreters Theatre." It would be helpful especially for education students planning to use storytelling or choral reading as curricular devices to teach English or reading at various elementary or secondary school levels. Those in a directing emphasis will find this textbook helpful in staging and creating production concepts for "presentational" theatrical events.

I have attempted to continue the personal and direct writing style first introduced in my other Kendall/Hunt textbook, *Communicating Literature: An Introduction to Oral Interpretation* (4th Edition). At the end of each chapter you will find discussion questions and assignments for you, your professor, and your peers in the class to consider. I have also attempted to help professors with possible student learning outcomes objectives at the end of Chapter 1.

As in my oral interpretation textbook, I am committed to the emphasis that the group performance of all texts needs to have a communicative intent. As I have said before, "each performance text should have an argument, a thesis, a premise, a theme, or a communicative center. Identifying this communicative center and making performance choices is what this text is all about" as well.[1]

Chapter 1 has clarifying definitions of Readers Theatre (RT) as well as distinctions between RT and conventional theatre. The chapter also has a history and development of group performance as well as an overview to the entire textbook. Chapter 2 establishes a "communicative theory" of group performance and the interactive elements of a model that ultimately lead to a response from any audience. Chapter 3 gives suggestions for selecting and analyzing the performance text. While some texts have obscure reasons for existence or message, the script producer must have an understanding of character, plot, theme development, and direction prior to any public presentation. Chapter 4 offers up brief reviews of verbal and nonverbal performance choices as well as discussions of focus, entrances/exits, and other theatrical accoutrements to be used during a performance. Chapters 5 and 6 give practical advice about line divisions and other performance variables in various literary and oral texts. Chapter 7 provides concepts for design and staging of presentational group performances in a variety of performance spaces. Chapter 8 is an attempt to explore the amorphous quality of "creativity" in generating ideas for performance. Practitioners and producers of readers theatre will offer insights into how each of them explores "new ways" to stage texts. This chapter is rather unique since most other group performance textbooks do not directly explore this topic. Chapter 9 has a dual purpose: (1) specific criteria for a production guide plus script required for all students in the course; (2) rehearsal strategies and plans leading up to the actual initial and continuing group performance of texts. Chapter 10 concludes the book with practical outlets for group performance, not merely in academic settings, but in religious centers, political events, social services, and advocacy guilds. In the Appendix you will find tear-out sample script sheets for classroom exercises, "creativity" exercises, group adaptation of texts opportunities, and evaluation sheets for peer-grading of in-class presentations.

You may find that the chapter order does not necessarily fit with the outline for your course. You should feel free to read chapters out of sequence and perhaps your professor will assign them in a different order. For example, some professors may wish to discuss the "creativity" issues prior to a chapter on design and staging of texts.

I want to follow the guideline I first used in the oral interpretation textbook and provide a few literary or created texts to provide opportunities to experience the thrill of learning while doing as I did. Sometimes I will ask you to divide up the lines and adapt the text; other times I will merely ask you to assign the lines within a group and practice to perform it in class sessions.

When I was first hired to teach at Biola University in 1974, I was able to discover how to put my graduate degree experiences into practice by creating many readers theatre 25-minute scripts for the competitive realm of forensics competition. For 20 years our Biola RT teams successfully offered up literary texts for consideration and pondering. So I am one who strongly endorses the meaningful outlet of forensics competition and festival offerings in group performance. That being said, I note that over the years the RT or Interpreters Theatre event has evolved from rigid rules and prescriptive formats to a more exciting theatrical endeavor. The American Readers Theatre Association (ARTa) has fostered a growth in creativity in the first years of the twenty-first century that has revitalized the art form. I know that in many four-year colleges and universities the group performance class is usually an upper division course, but many community colleges now also offer it as an elective course. I believe that community college instructors and students will find a mix of description and practical advice for performance, even if the actual creation of a production guide is beyond the scope of a lower division collegiate course.

I would like to thank the following colleagues for advice and for encouraging me over the years to complete this project: Kate Brandon, Biola University (CA); Erick Roebuck, Biola University (CA); Thomas Carmody, Vanguard University (CA); Michael Leigh, Orange Coast College (CA); Liesel Reinhart, Mount San Antonio College (CA); Dewi Hokett and Mark Newman, Palomar College (CA); Terry Petersen, Chabot College (CA); Lianna Koeppel-Taylor, Cypress College (CA); Larry Schnoor, University of Minnesota, Mankato; Diana Crossman, El Camino College (CA); and Raymond "Bud" Zeuschner, Cal Poly San Luis Obispo. Once again I thank my oldest son, Jonathan Price, for the cover design and internal graphic elements for models and figures in this edition. I would also like to offer my appreciation to Janice Samuells, Associate Editor, and Amanda Smith, Project Coordinator, with Kendall/Hunt Publishing Company for their help and assistance in this long-anticipated project. I know that I could not presume to write a textbook on Readers Theatre without thanking the hundreds of students who over the years have given of their talents and performance expertise in performing my adapted RT scripts.

I began with my story. Now it is time for you to begin your "story." If you think that your "story" needs to be told to others in a performance arena, you could discover how to adapt your own "oral" tradition to the compelling world of presentational theatre. If your "story" is best shared by others' words, I invite you to find those words and the means to bring them to life in an exciting endeavor for performance: Readers Theatre.

TODD V. LEWIS

References

1. Todd V. Lewis, *Communicating Literature: An Introduction to Oral Interpretation* (4th Edition). (Dubuque, IA: Kendall/Hunt Publishing Company, 2004), ix.

1

Readers Theatre: What Is It?

Introduction

When you think about witnessing a "theatrical event," you immediately envision entering an arena with seats scattered across the spectator space. You find your seat and look straight ahead to see possibly a curtain on a stage or perhaps a pre-set scene with furniture and decorations. You anticipate the lowering of the lights or the raising of the curtain to begin the play. Your responsibility as a "witness" to this event is to place your trust in an ensemble of actors who will attempt to entertain and/or educate you as they represent their art form.

But this is not the only scenario for observing or even performing a "theatrical event." One unique performative group art form does not require a pre-set stage (although it does not preclude it). This art form has no boundaries limited by a proscenium stage. This group art form is not limited to the presentation of texts that are written in dialogic dramatic play format. This different group art form has many names: Platform Theatre, Group Interpretation, Group Performance of Literature, Chamber Theatre, Theatre of the Word, or Interpreter's Theatre. But its most common historical name is Readers Theatre.

Note that Readers Theatre has no apostrophe; thus, it cannot be merely the "possession" of one or several performers. And furthermore, the group performance may not even hint or suggest that anyone is "reading" anything, since it could very well be memorized without visible texts or performance notebooks. "Readers" references those in the audience who have chosen to push their imaginations to the limit as "witnesses," much like those who give in to their imaginations as they read a text silently.

Once limited in a conventional, rule-based format that required stools, bare stage, a few nondescript boxes for sitting or standing, and of course, a scripted notebook, contemporary Readers Theatre has no such boundaries. *There is no right or exclusive way to present Readers Theatre.* And there is no limitation by venue or location for Readers Theatre (RT). Where any "space" is found, there a group can perform RT.

Definition

Readers Theatre is very much like the hybrid plant or more recently the hybrid automobile. RT implies that two or more *performers* present verbally and nonverbally a scripted *text* (e.g., prose, poetry, drama, nonfiction literature, ethnographies, oral tradition) to an *audience* capable of *re-creating* the words they hear onto the stage of their minds, so that all involved can consider the persuasive intent of the *message*. This presentation may be stark or elaborately theatrical. Readers Theatre emphasizes that what you hear need not be actually seen in order to become real. On the other hand, a fully costumed and theatrically embellished presentation may still be considered Readers Theatre. So what makes Readers Theatre a hybrid art form?

Readers *Theatre* recognizes that mere reading aloud cannot easily sustain audience interest or fuel the imagination. Movement and inter-relationships with other performers, multimedia (music, PowerPoint, video, DVD, film), costuming or group ensemble dress, and other theatrical accoutrements must *synergize* to bring a performed text to a life of its own. (*Synergy* conceptualizes that the total effect of independent agencies working together is greater than the sum of each individual effect.) It is the contemporary "theatrical," which has rescued RT from the doldrums of conventional inertia. RT does not consist of boringly sitting on stools and reading aloud with little vocal inflection or movement.

Readers Theatre also wants the performance of any text to accomplish more than mere entertainment. RT should encourage audiences to think and sometimes change behavior (possibly attitudes) and not just emotionally respond to a theatrical event. Any performed text should have a clear message to communicate.

Readers Theatre: A Definition

Readers Theatre implies that two or more *performers* present verbally and nonverbally a scripted *text* of any literary or oral genre to an *audience* capable of *re-creating* the words they hear onto the stage of their minds, so that all involved can consider the persuasive intent of the *message*.

Figure 1.1

This text is committed to the hybrid nature of Readers Theatre. Its threefold nature comprises: *readers* (performers), *texts* (not merely those in dramatic format), and an *audience* capable of discerning a message. Readers Theatre is not superior or inferior to conventional drama. It is another performable art form.

Performable art forms frequently overlap, blurring any real distinctions. However, most conventional drama requires that the text be scripted into dramatic dialogue (wherein exposition is discovered). RT has no restrictions, nor does the text have to be dialogic in format. Readers can "dramatize" narrative portions of nondramatic literature. Most (yet not all) conventional drama asks an audience to "eavesdrop" through an invisible fourth wall. Most RT presentations (yet not all) break down the *fourth wall* to present the text directly to the audience. Most (yet not all) conventional drama requires a *pictorial space*: boxed-in, limited performance area, usually with sets and curtains, lighting, and theatrically *actualized* reality. RT may use pictorial space, but can also be offered in *acoustic* or *found space*: the whole environment, including the audience's mind. Conventional Theatre usually strives to *represent* reality; RT usually strives to *present* some sort of imagined reality.

Other distinctions between Readers Theatre and Conventional Theatre abound. The presence of visible scripts is optional in RT, the absence of scripts is a norm in conventional theatre. Actors stay on stage without literal exits or entrances (RT); actors walk on and off of a stage in conventional theatre. Readers Theatre allows for the option of having a performer play more than one character; conventional theatre usually has primary actors playing one role exclusively. The spectacle elements of a Readers Theatre are most often suggested; the spectacle elements of conventional theatre are literally offered.

The third aspect for Readers Theatre, the audience, has a crucial participatory role. It is a different role than that for most conventional theatre audiences. The audience role for much of any theatrical event labeled as "Readers Theatre" must embrace what Leslie Irene Coger called "double vision":

> They [the audience members] see the interpreters
> onstage before them, but superimposed over them
> they view the characters interacting in the world of
> the literature.[1]

One can call a theatrical event "Readers Theatre" if some portion of the event calls for the audience to use its individual mind to focus on performed text and the imagined scene. It now makes sense that Readers Theatre has also been labeled as "Theatre of the Mind."

Distinctions between Readers Theatre and Most Conventional Theatre	
Readers Theatre	**Conventional Theatre**
Actors May or May Not Have Visible Scripts	Usually Memorized
Actors Stay on Stage (No Literal Entrances/Exits)	Actors Walk On/Off Stage
Multiple Characters per Actor Possible	Usually One Actor per Role
Scenes Re-created in the Mind	Scenes Actualized Onstage
Minimally Staged or Theatricalized	Staged with Realistic Set
Message Plus Entertainment in Text	Entertainment Preeminent
Any Literature or Text Presented	Only Dramatic Literature
Usually Some Direct Eye Contact with Audience	Usually Fourth Wall in Place
Presentational	Representational
Spectacle Elements Are Suggested	Spectacle Elements Are Literal
Can Use Found/Acoustic Space	Uses Pictorial Space
"Theatre of the Mind"	"Theatre for the Stage"

Figure 1.2

History and Development of Readers Theatre

Historic group reading or recitation practices precede modern Readers Theatre practice. Storytellers or *rhapsodes* were reciting with dramatic flair the works of Greek poets in public performances during the fifth Century BC. Choral reading or recitation was a theatrical element not only in the classical Greek and Roman theatre but also in medieval mystery plays. As early as the tenth century AD, a German nun named

Hroswitha wrote plays about biblical characters and saints, intending these plays to be more presentational than actualized, read aloud by group members rather than acted out. Hroswitha was educated in the secular spheres of an aristocratic wealthy family, but when she chose to become a cloistered nun, the bawdy content of the Roman plays she loved to read seemed inappropriate in a religious setting. However, she discovered she could bridge the gap between the secular and the sacred by using the same playwriting format as the Romans, but not succumbing to the nature of secular actualized scene performance. In a sense, Hroswitha is the "great grandmother" of modern Readers Theatre.[2]

"Closet Dramas," plays not written for theatrical presentation, but rather for private social hour readings, were popular in the nineteenth century in both England as well as the United States. A particular group presentation format that was well received in the 1920s, first in England and than later in America, was the Verse Choir or Choral Reading. Poetry tends to be the primary literature for this kind of presentation and many educational curricular programs continue to make use of this format today.[3] The term "Readers Theatre" was probably first used in the 1930s by a U.S.A. government—sponsored "welfare supportive" organization called "The Group Theatre," who sponsored play readings by unemployed New York actors. The term "Readers Theatre" was revisited to describe a New York City production of Sophocles' *Oedipus Rex* that apparently relied on static performers reading from behind lecterns.[4] In 1951, well-known stage and film actor Charles Laughton convinced director Paul Gregory to mount a staged reading of the Hell scenes from George Bernard Shaw's play, *Man and Superman*. Re-named "Don Juan in Hell," these scenes were rarely staged because the proscenium theatre seemed inadequate to conceptualize it and the entire Shaw play was much too long for audiences. Laughton was joined by his contemporaries Charles Boyer, Agnes Moorehead, and Sir Cedric Hardwicke, offering a "group reading" (stools and lecterns) not merely for an appreciative Broadway crowd, but on a tour to many other states as well.[5]

Gregory followed up this "new" approach to theatre with an even bolder venture in 1953: dramatizing nondramatic literature in *John Brown's Body*, an epic poem by Stephen Vincent Benét. The free-verse poetic lines were divided between three actors (Tyrone Power, Dame Judith Anderson, and Raymond Massey) and the show was quite successful and revived in 1968–1969 and 1971–1972.[6]

Many other professional productions incorporated the concepts and techniques of Readers Theatre, but rarely if ever identified a production by that name. Gradually, people moved out and away from stools and lecterns to dance, sing, and chorally respond to highly theatrical, yet still "presentational" theatre. Productions in the 1950s and 1960s of this type included: *John dos Passos' USA, God's Trombones, Spoon River Anthology, In White America; A Whitman Portrait;* and *A Thurber Carnival.*[7]

No longer are professional productions of nondramatic literature seen as oddities. Conventional Theatre has embraced the traditions of Readers Theatre and contributed an unlimited freedom to explore varying creative approaches to presentational theatre. From the musical *You're a Good Man, Charlie Brown* (1967; 1999) to the Royal Shakespeare Company's epic two-night/two-ticket eight-hour venue of Charles Dickens' *Nicholas Nickleby* (1982), presentational theatre is alive and well professionally on Broadway and elsewhere.[8] Finding its initial run in off-Broadway smaller venues, A. R. Gurney's *Love Letters* is basically a Readers Theatre program for two people who read and exchange letters over a lifetime. Frequently new actors come in for each performance of this highly presentational contemporary "play."

Learning his craft as a professor of Readers Theatre at Northwestern University, Frank Galati won a director/adaptor Tony Award in 1990 for his professional Readers Theatre-like adaptation of John Steinbeck's novel, *The Grapes of Wrath*. In 1992 and 1993 Homer's epic poem *The Odyssey* was produced by the Royal Shakespeare Company and presented in London, New York City, and Washington, DC. It was performed on a "bare stage, to evoke ancient empires with only words and a few props."[9] During the 1993 theatrical season in London, a stage adaptation of Graham Greene's 1969 novel, *Travels With My Aunt* won Olivier Awards. The staging and adaptation were essentially Readers Theatre with four males, identically dressed, performing multiple character roles, both male and female (and even a dog), while focusing onstage glances as well as presentational direct eye contact with the audience. Also in London, Stephen Mallatrott's adaptation of *The Woman in Black*, a two-act compilation of ghost stories, may be the longest running (18 years, still in production as of this publication) Readers Theatre in history.[10]

In 1975 a group of professional actors, writers, educators, and singers created *The Open Book*, New York City's first professional Readers Theatre ensemble. This group has continued to perform a wide variety of genres and even "oral" texts with the usual RT devices plus "controlled dynamics and multiple rhythms associated with chamber or choral music," identified as "The Open Book effect."[11]

But no doubt the greatest growth in Readers Theatre interest began to happen in the 1960s in academic, particularly collegiate, environments. If Hroswitha can be considered the "great grandmother" of modern Readers Theatre, then the true heir and "mother" figure would have to be Leslie Irene Coger of Southwest Missouri State University. Coger cowrote the seminal *Readers Theatre Handbook* with Melvin R. White of Brooklyn College, and until it went out of print after three decades of use, it was the "bible" for Readers Theatre instruction and practice.[12] Even after her death in 1999 at the age of 87, she continues to influence creativity in Readers Theatre productions in academic settings. Continuing this familial metaphor, The Institute for Readers Theatre in San Diego, California, named radio producer, Norman Corwin as the "Father of Readers Theatre" for his decades of creativity and promotion for the "theatre of the imagination."[13]

Since the mid-1970s Readers Theatre has made creative and theatrical strides in the competitive arena of college forensics tournaments. Incorporated into the event listings at the community college national tournament (Phi Ro Pi), RT has also now come into its own as an exclusive national conference and tournament event for all colleges and universities. ARTa, the American Readers Theatre Association, sponsored its first conference and tournament in May of 2001, hosted by Mount San Antonio College in Walnut, California. ARTa now attracts colleges and universities from all over the United States to its May event, with upwards of twenty RT offerings presented annually. More than a competition, the conference gathering has training sessions and dialogue opportunities with directors and collegiate performers from varying backgrounds and experiences.

Both professionally and academically RT is healthy and evolving as an art form. No longer merely the purview of Broadway or the university stage, RT is being used to teach, instruct, and even lead worship in religious settings.[14] Also, the late William Adams, founder of the Institute for Readers Theatre, began a training conference for directors to take and adapt texts for curricular offerings in elementary and secondary schools as well as advocacy groups in social services (e.g., unions, libraries, recreational clubs, senior citizen homes, programs for the disabled).[15]

Overview of the Book

If you are taking a class in Readers Theatre, Interpreter's Theatre, or some form of group performance, you should have several learning outcomes. First, you will understand the theoretical basis for communicating a message to an audience by means of a group performance. Second, you should have opportunities to learn how to adapt various genres of literary texts and even "oral" texts for use in performance. Third, you should gain experience in experimentation with various and creative group performance staging arrangements. Fourth, you should be able to compose a production guide with performance text as well as staging designs, useful for one who may choose to direct a specific production. Fifth, you should increase your own performable skills as an actor in this presentational format. And finally, you should become aware of the many outlets for RT presentations in your expanding communities and interest groups. While the "learning" can certainly come from studying for a classroom examination or quizzes, the true "learning" in this course comes from the "doing" of the art form.

Readers Theatre is truly alive, well, and flourishing. Your tasks ahead of you may lead to performance, adaptation, and directing of theatricalized texts—and hopefully all of these. There is no age limit, no space restriction, no narrow rules on what RT can be or where and what it can offer. Excitement and wonder and sobering thought await you as you explore the creative art form known as Readers Theatre.

Discussion and Assignments

1. Name a "conventional" theatre presentation you recently watched and discuss how the actors maintained the allusion of the "fourth wall."

2. Name, if you can, a "Readers Theatre-like" theatre presentation you recently watched and discuss how the actors broke down the "fourth wall" and engaged the audience.

3. Was there any noticeable sense that you as an audience member were expected to play a different role in each type of theatrical presentation? Why or why not?

4. Though virtually all theatre desires to entertain, name a play you watched recently that seemed more message-oriented than mere entertainment. How did the playwright "share" this message through dialogue?

5. Name a piece of literature or an oral text you recently read or heard that has a very clear "message" to it. Why was it compelling to you? What elements within the text could you envision being adapted into a performable text?

6. Begin a survey of texts and materials you might choose to include in a Readers Theatre Production Guide, due later in the course. Keep copies of these materials in a separate file, folder, or notebook for reference at a later date.

7. Your instructor may desire to "skill test" your individual performing ability, so you should bring a brief textual performance piece (3–5 minutes) to class in a week and be prepared to present it from a notebook or completely memorized in front of your class audience.

8. If your instructor has access to previously performed Readers Theatre scripts and provides you with one, read it prior to the next class meeting and come prepared to discuss its "presentational" elements.

Additional Reading

Kleinau, Marion L., and McHughes, Janet Larsen. *Theatres for Literature.* Sherman Oaks, CA: Alfred Publishing Company, Inc., 1980.

Lewis, Todd V. "Chapter 11: Readers Theatre and Other Group Forms of Interpretation." *Communicating Literature: An Introduction to Oral Interpretation,* 4th Edition. Dubuque, IA: Kendall/Hunt Publishing Company, 2004.

Long, Beverly Whitaker; Hudson, Lee; and Jeffrey, Phillis Rienstra. *Group Performance of Literature.* Englewood Cliffs, NJ: Prentice-Hall, Inc., 1977.

Ratliff, Gerald Lee. *Introduction to Readers Theatre: A Guide to Classroom Performance.* Colorado Springs, CO: Meriwether Publishing Ltd., 1999.

Tanner, Fran Averett. *Readers Theatre Fundamentals.* Caldwell, ID: Clark Publishing Company, 1987.

Yordon, Judy E. *Experimental Theatre: Creating and Staging Texts.* Prospect Heights, IL: Waveland Press, Inc., 1997.

References

1. Leslie Irene Coger and Melvin R. White, *Readers Theatre Handbook* (Glenview, IL: Scott, Foresman, and Company, 1982), 13.

2. Todd V. Lewis, "Hroswitha: Precursor of Religious Readers Theatre," *Religious Communication Today*, 7 (September 1984): 35–39.

3. Eugene Bahn and Margaret L. Bahn, *A History of Oral Interpretation*. Minneapolis: Burgess Publishing Company, 1970), 173.

4. Judy E. Yordon, "Preface," in Marvin Kaye, *From Page to Stage* (Garden City, NY: The Fireside Theatre, 1996), vii.

5. Alice Barnhart, ed., "Paul Gregory Speaks," *Readers Theatre News* (Winter 1974): 3.

6. Mary Frances HopKins and Brent Bouldin, "Professional Group Performance of Nondramatic Literature in New York," in David W. Thompson, ed., *Performances of Literature in Historical Perspectives*. (Lanham, MD: University Press of America, 1983), 699.

7. HopKins and Bouldin, 700–709.

8. William Adams, *Institute Book for Readers Theatre: A Practical Guide for School, Theater, & Community* (Chapel Hill, NC: Professional Press, 2003), 239.

9. Richard Corliss, "Club Adriatic," a review of *The Odyssey, TIME* (October 31, 1994): 78.

10. Adams, *Institute Book for Readers Theatre*, 257.

11. Marvin Kaye, ed., *Readers Theatre* (Newark, NJ: Wildside Press, 1995), 11.

12. Coger and White, *Readers Theatre Handbook* (Glenview, IL: Scott, Foresman, and Company, 1967, 1973, 1982).

13. Adams, *Institute Book for Readers Theatre*, 234–235.

14. Todd V. Lewis, *RT: A Readers Theatre Ministry* (Kansas City, MO: Lillenas Publishing Company, 1988) and Gordon C. Bennett, *Readers Theatre Comes to Church* (Colorado Springs, CO: Meriwether Publishing Ltd., 1972, 1985).

15. Adams, *Institute Book for Readers Theatre*, 279–294.

2

Transforming Texts Into Group Performance: Theory and Perceptions

Communicative Intent of Texts in Performance

A primary philosophical assumption of this textbook is that a performable text has a communicative message or intent. Every text has an intrinsic message that can and should influence performers and audiences alike. Finding or discovering textual intent is not always easy, apparent, nor possibly knowable. So why be committed to this investigation into textual analysis?

While scholars disagree as to whether **any author's intent** is even knowable, there is general consensus that the **group** performance of texts *is simultaneously an art as well as a communicative act.* Wallace Bacon recognized that the performance of literature

> may be given a specific rhetorical or forensics slant;
> it may select one dominant attitude from a piece and
> emphasize that...to make a particular point a reader
> or a program may wish to stress.[1]

But Bacon cautions those who look exclusively for rhetorical messages that literary texts cannot be reduced to merely what they "say" or "tell." For Bacon and many scholars a literary text lives and evolves as directors and performers engage it.[2]

Contemporary performance theory proposes that when literary or author intent may be elusive or unknowable, a critical "dialogue" can still occur. This dialogue is far different than studying the verbal interactions of characters in a dramatized text. It is a dialogue process beginning with any text itself and how that text is never complete or finished:

> It also suggests that every text is connected to other texts, that every text, in some sense, *reads* or *speaks* to other texts, drawing connections, that are both obvious and indirect.[3]

This analytical approach to examining oral and literary texts is called *intertextuality*. Soviet critic Mikhail Bakhtin argues that this dialogism among an author, an adaptor, a performance director, a performer, even an audience alters what any text could mean at any given moment of time.[4]

Bakhtin called this process *heteroglossia* or "different tongues/languages overlayed and linked to any other text." Whether you use the term *intertextuality* or *heteroglossia*, the critical assumption assumes that all texts have fluid meanings.

Postmodern philosophical influences also lead to assumptions that all interpretations of intent or rhetorical messages have equal validity. All "stories" are equal.[5] It is the fundamental assumption of this textbook that while *any text may have many interpretations, not all choices for interpretation are wise*. If any text can as a result of the dialogic process mean everything, then one must grant that any text is *meaningless* since it becomes devoid of uniqueness or common communicative understanding.

A more pragmatic approach to intertextuality contends that the dialogic process that generates multiple interpretations creates *choices*, some supportable, some provocative, some nuanced, some downright weird or untenable.[6]

Intertextuality?

The Changed Man
Robert Phillips

If you were to hear me imitating Pavarotti
in the shower every morning, you would know
how much you have changed my life.

If you were to see me stride across the park,
waving to stranger, then you would know
I am a changed man—like Scrooge

awakened from his bad dreams feeling feather-
light, angel-happy, laughing the father
of a long line of bright laughs—

"It is still not too late to change my life!"
It is changed. Me, who felt short-changed.
Because of you I no longer hate my body.

Because of you I buy new clothes.
Because of you I'm a warrior of joy.
Because of you and me. Drop by

this Saturday morning and discover me
fiercely pulling weeds gladly, dedicated
as a born-again gardener.

Drop by on Sunday—I'll Turtlewax
your sky-blue sports car, no sweat. I'll greet
enemies with a handshake, forgive debtors

with a papal largesse. It's all because
of you. Because of you and me,
I've become one changed man.

Phillips, Robert. *Spinach Days*. pp. 50 © 2000 by Robert Phillips.
Reprinted by permission of The Johns Hopkins University Press.

What are some possible theoretical and critical methods to generate the list of choices for finding intertextual meaning? John Creagh articulates three such methods useful for the performer, the adaptor/director, even the audience for group performance. The *objectivist view* looks only at the text itself or reports concerning the text, but may overlook the text as experience. The *dramatistic view*, espoused by rhetorician Kenneth Burke and others, attributes motives in contexts, but may ignore interpersonal reactions to a text. The *speech act approach* or *reader-oriented attribution* criticism embraces the dialogic/interpersonal approach of intertextuality and the resulting interpretive alternatives.[7]

These critical methodologies are certainly not the only means to generate possible textual meanings or choices. But the activity of textual analysis, laying out the choices, is crucially important for ensemble performer, adaptor/director, and the audience.

Any sensitive, self-assured director of a group performance will encourage dialogue with his/her cast about "choices." "Make a strong choice in your characterization," you will hear. "I liked that choice better than last time," you may also hear. Yes, all texts can have multiple interpretations, but a wise performer, adaptor/director, or audience embraces the strongest choice. Stern and Henderson conclude:

> Perhaps choice is the hallmark of a balanced approach,
> for although choice may inevitably mean moving to
> one way of performing a text at a given moment, it also
> means becoming consciously aware of the alternatives
> and knowing your reasons for selecting one set of
> options over another in a specified context.[8]

We will explore this notion of intertextuality once again in Chapter 3 as we look at juxtaposing multiple texts in performance and the resulting alteration of context. Notions of intertextuality need not lead to the "death of any author's intent," but hopefully the unraveling of textual layering brought about by interaction with other texts.

Presentational Theory Notions: Alienation Devices

Conventional Theatre and Readers Theatre share much in common,
yet are unique art forms (as you learned in Chapter 1). Experimental
playwrights/directors Bertolt Brecht and Thornton Wilder instituted
a number of mechanisms to make their conventional theatre offerings
more presentational. These mechanisms, called *alienation devices*, have
been incorporated into many Readers Theatre productions.

Alienation from Brecht's and Wilder's perspective is not a negative
factor. They certainly did not want to antagonize an audience or push
them away from embracing a performance. Quite the opposite, Brecht
and Wilder use the term *alienation* to break with traditional staging
and engage the audience presentationally and directly. The alienation
effect for Brecht would prevent the audience from becoming emotionally attached to the characters only. Since Brecht's plays were highly
politicized, he chose to alienate traditions so that audiences would
think about and possibly be persuaded to endorse his political agenda.
Here are some prominent alienation devices, now frequently incorporated into Readers Theatre productions:

1. *Use of narrator:* Wilder makes the narrator a unique character
   in his play, *Our Town*. This character breaks down the convention of the "fourth wall" and talks directly to the audience.
   Such a narrator can serve as a bridge between scenes with stark
   or minimal scene settings. Brecht might use his narrator to set
   a scene or even comment about and interpret a scene with a
   political nuance for the audience.

2. *Use of scripts/notebooks:* Although the presence of scripts or
   three-ring binder notebooks is optional, their presence reminds
   the audience that a text should receive some focus as well as the
   actions of a group of performers. Having a script present may
   also be useful as a prop. Creative performers may implement the
   script as a steering wheel, a letter, a baby, a wall component,
   or any other imagined object or action.

21

3. **Stage filled with nondescript properties:** Boxes, chairs, ladders, steps, and non-specific set pieces comprise a staged area. Their mobility and multiuse lead audiences to imagine the setting rather than witness it in reality.

4. **Audience focus:** Not merely the narrator but performers address the audience on occasion with direct eye contact, breaking down the fourth wall. Performers can even enter or exit the performance space from the realm of the audience.

5. **Offstage focus:** Two or more characters in dialogue will look above the heads of the audience to "see" the other. The audience should understand that the dialogue is not with them, but with the "imagined" other. It is as if a conventional scene was cut down the middle of eye gaze and rotated and presentationally offered to an engaged audience. An audience now has the ability to see facial expressions fully rather than side-to-side interactions.

6. **Mime or suggested movement replaces actual activities:** Audiences will imagine suggested movement and replace it in their minds with a completed sense of what is offered. Complex activities can be suggested without actual demonstrations.

7. **Performers may portray more than one character:** By moving location in a scene, altering vocal and nonverbal patterns, or adding/subtracting costume features, performers can become more than one character or role.

8. **Multiple performers may portray one character:** Called *bifurcation*, two performers may represent inner or outward attitudes or complexity of personality. *Trifurcation* uses three performers to portray one persona. (This was notably used in the 1993 London production, *Travels With My Aunt*).

9. *Multimedia accompanies live action performance:* Performers may act out a scene while slides, PowerPoint, video, film, or live performed music occurs simultaneously onstage with them.

10. *Ensemble costuming may not be literal, but color-coordinated:* Ensemble dressing represents the notion that color and uniformity are more important than actualized reality. A uniform dressed appearance can suggest one-for-many or many-for-one notions.

Presentational Theory Notions: Psychological Closure

I remember the first Readers Theatre script I produced. Called "The Voyeurism of Violence," I found this poignant short story concerning a troubled teenager who crawled out a church window high above the sidewalk.[9] This story was to be the script's centerpiece. A narrative described the suicidal youth's venture to the base of the church steeple. Dialogue portions revealed an initial caring crowd, but as time proceeds the frustrated crowd changes to an angry mob, calling out to the youth to jump and get it finished. The youth wavers, then plummets to the ground. The crowd disperses, callously claiming, "Kid's gonna jump — you can't stop him."

I did not need to actualize a youth falling from a great height to capture my audience's attention. I created the allusion of what was being described. Each performer looked upwards, focusing on the imaginary youth (in a location on the ceiling) and gradually dropped their eye gaze in slow motion until he "landed" on the "empty" space in front of them. They hovered around this empty space, another performer came and laid his script over the empty space as if it were a "blanket" and all performers walked away, turning their backs on the scene location.

Some audience members actually screamed, some cried. Why? They envisioned the details and filled in the missing actualized components by means of a device known as *psychological closure.*

Psychological closure occurs when a suggested action or reaction has a consistency and a sense of completion. Our brains will "close" or complete the perceived event if enough information is provided to suggest the process. Our brains do this when watching films or videos in which individual cinematic cels reveal partial movements and because of "persistence of vision" we perceive the whole, not the individual part. If you have a text with a phone, the imagined cell phone is picked up, cover flipped open, maybe handed to another, or rested on a shoulder (while you turn a script page, for example). The completed action might include closing the cell phone cover with a mimed action and placing "it" in a pocket. If someone "hands" you a drink, you must "receive" it in completed action. The psychological closure has been completed.

Psychological closure seems to also operate in other notions of Readers Theatre. Actual scenes that are stark or minimalist require closure to further the illusion. Multiple character roles by a single performer call for the imagined sense that each role is uniquely different.

This theoretical concept has been identified by other performance scholars as *behavioral synecdoche* (pronounced sin-EK-duh-key).[10] Synecdoche is a type of literary imagery, used as a device to show that the part can suggest the whole. For example, Francis Scott Key wrote this phrase in the American national anthem, "Whose broad stripes and bright stars..." as a synecdoche for the American flag.

Readers Theatre practitioners have embraced the metaphor of synecdoche and linked it to stage movement and actions in a performance. Full-blown movement as seen in conventional theatre has its equivalent in Readers Theatre's use of behavioral synecdoche. Minimal or economic movement *suggests* the whole in Readers Theatre productions.

24

Behavioral synecdoche is one of the key characteristic theoretical underpinnings for Readers Theatre as an art form, unique from most conventional theatre offerings. Audience members may not see one character actually "kiss" another character, but the simulation of kissing (using offstage focus and pursed lips) allows the audience to conceptualize the "whole" action by seeing its "part." Sometimes behavioral synecdoche can help conceptualize a scene by seeing one prop or a basic set-piece. Applications of this theoretical concept enliven the creativity for adaptation and performance of both oral and literary texts.

A Communication Model for Readers Theatre

The interaction between four components of a communication model for Readers Theatre has a parallel to the realm of persuasion and influence in the mass media. Such theoretical constructs as the *two-step flow of information* or the *multistep flow of information* remind us that "opinion leaders" or "gatekeepers" monitor, filter, and alter the perception/interpretation of what we hear, accept, and believe in the mass media.[11]

Two-Step Flow of Information Model
Message/Text ⇨ Opinion Leader/Gatekeeper ⇨ Audience

Multi-Step Flow of Information Model
Message/Text ⇨ Peers/Socioeconomic Factors, Etc. ⇨ Gatekeeper ⇨ Audience

Figure 2.1

Performers "grow" into parts and understand subtextual nuances as the rehearsal process continues. Even as rehearsals transition to actual performances, the performers may alter their performance choices slightly as new meanings for each text emerge. Some adaptor/directors will applaud these "growth" periods, complimenting performers on their insights. But there could also be occasions when performers need to be reminded of an earlier "vision" and recommit to the adaptor/director's "filtered" response to the performed text.

All performers share their own stories about certain audiences that respond with expected behaviors, as well as audiences who respond unpredictably. When the "unpredictable" becomes "routinized," then the performer must evaluate and ask if audiences are hearing something other than what was intended or prepared. Audiences have a profound impact on performers and adaptor/directors who may even further adapt their performance choices to highlight significant, ongoing responses. The audience that laughs at a line, not determined to be all that funny in rehearsals, can influence performance choices from that point on.

This current model has at its center the rehearsal process. The adaptor/director comes to the first rehearsal with a production concept that includes a rationale for why the text has a message and what that message should be. This adaptor/director shares the "vision" of this message with a cast of performers who begin to be stimulated by the text and performance options for this chosen message. Interpersonal dialogue occurs and is called "analysis." (More will be said about "analysis" in Chapter 3.) From the outset of rehearsals the anticipated audience may be small, made up of a director, possibly a few support personnel, but also the performers, whether performing at the time or not. All comprise the "test" audience. There may be a "dress rehearsal" with a slightly large self-selected audience. Then, the rehearsal period terminates; the text and the "vision" are ready for public presentation.

During the performance stage, the four component features expand the interaction to the perimeters of the model and the realm of public presentation. Hopefully, the text stimulates the audience by means of the artistry of the original adaptor, the director, and the skills of the performers.

As the process unfolds, the location of the literary experience, the locus of the text, should be primarily in the minds of any audience. The "vision," once only in the mind of the adaptor/director, was passed on to the minds of the performers, who in turn now have the exhilarating opportunity to do all in their power to implant that "vision" in a recreating process within the minds of an audience. Imagination is given free rein and the creativity of this art form is experienced.

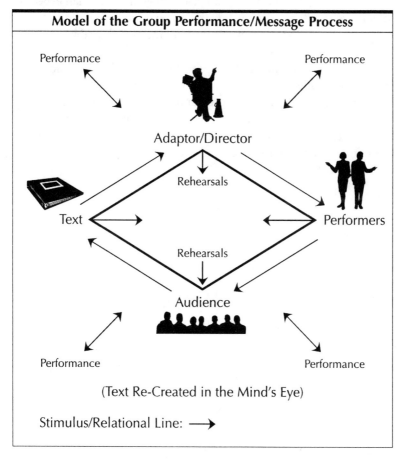

Model of the Group Performance/Message Process

Performance

Performance

Adaptor/Director

Rehearsals

Text ⟷ Performers

Rehearsals

Audience

Performance

Performance

(Text Re-Created in the Mind's Eye)

Stimulus/Relational Line: ⟶

Figure 2.2

Conclusion

Having a commitment to the shared message of a central or created performance text can be exciting, intriguing, and certainly imaginative. But caution must exist as well. Forcing a text to persuade or share a message through manipulations, omissions, even performance choices, distorts the performance activity. Weaker and unwise performance choices lead to poor acting, misunderstandings, and less than expected interactive results. The re-created literary experience, placed in the minds of an audience, may not be as fulfilling as it should be.

On the other hand, when text, adaptor/director, performers, and audience come together in a balanced, mutually respectful, and insightful performance, excellence is achieved and impact is sensed and experienced. Humanity is blessed, our cultures are affirmed, and we all grow and mature in our quest to understand the complexities of the human condition—all due to the study and witness of the group performance of literary texts.

Discussion and Assignments

1. If you have not done so already, purchase a solid cover (dark blue or black) three-ring binder notebook. Office supply stores or school bookstores may have the 7 by 9 inch size. It is easy to cradle this kind of notebook in one hand if necessary. Bring it to class on days when binder notebooks will be useful for class exercises.

2. Divide the class into groupings of two or three. Bring your 7 by 9 inch three-ring binder notebooks with you. List and demonstrate at least five different ways that the binder could symbolize or stand for a "prop" in performing a literary text. Take 6–8 minutes, than provide your report to the class as a whole. How can "script as prop" serve as an "alienation device" during a Readers Theatre performance?

3. Study the intertextual overlays and references found in Robert Phillips' "The Changed Man" poem on page 19. Discuss with members of your class which allusions and connections are necessary to understand in order to create a best possible choice scenario for performance.

4. You will find Robert Phillips' poem duplicated in the Appendix as an exercise for you and your classmates. Randomly divide into groups of two or three and divide the lines of the poem into lines for one, two, or all three readers. Tear out the page, place it in your notebook, and present at least two versions of the poem in a group presentation within your class.

5. Name several categories for intertextuality (i.e., categories of literary allusions and their original source). Besides the Bible or Shakespeare, what other sources influence literary or even oral tradition references?

6. Keep reading and filing possible literary selections for later use in your production guide. Check out unusual sources (e.g., children's literature, newspaper editorials, documentaries, etc.).

7. If you have access to a DVD or video tape of a Readers Theatre, watch it in class. Following the viewing, discuss the uses of psychological closure and behavioral synecdoche in the production. What was effective? Why? What needed more assistance for your imagination? Why?

Additional Reading

Gray, Paul H., and VanOosting, James. *Performances in Life and Literature.* Boston: Allyn and Bacon, 1996.

Haas, Richard and Williams, David A., eds. *The Study of Oral Interpretation: Theory and Comment.* Indianapolis: Bobbs-Merrill Company, Inc., 1975.

Lewis, Todd V. "Chapter 3: Communicating Literature: Theory and Perceptions." *Communicating Literature: An Introduction to Oral Interpretation*—4th Edition. Dubuque, IA: Kendall/Hunt Publishing Company, 2004.

Long, Beverly Whitaker; Hudson, Lee; and Jeffrey, Phillis Rienstra. *Group Performance of Literature.* Englewood Cliffs, NJ: Prentice-Hall, Inc., 1977.

Maclay, Joanna Hawkins. *Readers Theatre; Toward a Grammar of Practice.* New York: Random House, Inc., 1971.

References

1. Wallace A. Bacon, *The Art of Interpretation*—3rd Edition. (New York: Holt, Rinehart and Winston, 1979), 451.

2. Bacon, "The Dangerous Shores: A Decade Later," in Richard Haas and David A. Williams, eds. *The Study of Oral Interpretation: Theory and Comment.* (Indianapolis: The Bobbs-Merrill Company, Inc., 1975), 227.

3. Carol Simpson Stern and Bruce Henderson, *Performance: Texts and Contexts* (New York: Longman Publishing Group, 1993), 369.

4. See: Mikhail Bakhtin in *The Dialogic Imagination*, Michael Holquist, ed. Caryl Emerson and Michael Holquist, trans. (Austin: University of Texas Press, 1981).

5. See: Philip Auslander, *From Acting to Performance: Essays in Modernism and Postmodernism.* (New York: Routledge, 1997) and Steven Connor, *Postmodern Culture: An Introduction to Theories of the Contemporary*—2nd Edition. (Oxford, England and Cambridge, MA: B. Blackwell, 1997).

6. The process of determining better and best choices, applying the merits of various literary interpretations is called *hermeneutics*. See: John B. Thompson, *Critical Hermeneutics* (Cambridge: Cambridge University Press, 1981), 10.

7. John Creagh, "The Interpersonal Metaphor in Literary Criticism: Towards an Attribution-Based Model of Literary Response," *The Carolinas Speech Communication Annual*, 2 (1986): 15–23.

8. Stern and Henderson, *Performance*, 376.

9. Entitled "Incident on 49ᵗʰ Street" by Phyllis Reynolds Naylor, this story was a part of a collection of short stories published as *Dark Side of the Moon: Stories* (Philadelphia: Fortress Press, 1969). Naylor has become a prolific fiction writer for children and teenagers. This original collection is now out of print, but Naylor has many other novelettes and stories that reveal deep concerns for children as they relate to the world of adult living.

10. The first apparent use of this concept and terminology in relation to the performance of literature was by Don Geiger, "The Oral Interpreter as Creator," *The Speech Teacher*, 3 (November 1954): 275–276. See also: William R. Brown, Joseph Epolito, and Nancy Palmer Stump, "Genre Theory and the Practice of Readers Theatre," *The Speech Teacher*, 23 (January 1974): 1–8; Leslie Irene Coger and Melvin R. White, *Readers Theatre Handbook*—3ʳᵈ Edition. (Glenview, IL: Scott, Foresman and Company, 1982), 105; Fran A. Tanner, *Readers Theatre Fundamentals.* (Caldwell, ID: Clark Publishing Company, 1987), 18–19; Judy E. Yordon, *Experimental Theatre: Creating and Staging Texts.* (Prospect Heights, IL: Waveland Press, Inc., 1997), 7, 47, 82, 168.

3

Transforming Texts
Into Group Performance:
Selection and Analysis

The obvious expectation for any playwright is that a finished dramatic work must be performed. Gradually, we are beginning to sense that that expectation may also be true for other literary genres—prose fiction and nonfiction, poetry, and oral traditions. As Long, Hudson, and Jeffrey remind us, "these too, we believe, may reveal their fullest meaning through performance."[1]

With that philosophy in mind, this chapter provides assistance in text selection options for Readers Theatre and further develops pre-performance notions of analysis. We begin with establishing helpful criteria for choosing texts that best suit the Readers Theatre format to group performance.

Criteria for Text Selection

No listing of suitability for performance can be all inclusive, but beginning with a checklist will assist you in your search for performable texts:

1. *Does the text have vivid enriched language?*: Something in the language used attracted you initially to a text. Did you laugh at the humorous explanation of a situation? Did you shudder or sense fear because of the word pictures by an author? Were you compelled to make or consider a behavioral change because of the juxtaposition of words? Look for texts with vivid language. Consider this example:

> *Bodach* is a word that I heard a visiting six-year old English boy use to describe...a small, vile, and supposedly mythical beast of the British Isles, who comes down chimneys to carry off naughty children....He was the only person I have ever known who shared my special sight. Minutes after he spoke the word *bodach* in my presence, he was crushed to death between a runaway truck and a concrete black wall....When I was a child, I first thought that these shades might be malevolent spirits who fostered evil in those people around whom they swarmed. I've since discovered that many human beings need no supernatural mentoring to commit acts of savagery; some people are devils in their own right, their telltale horns having grown inward to facilitate their disguise.
>
> From *Old Thomas* by Dean Koontz, Bantam Books, 2003.

Dean Koontz is a prolific writer, choosing to explore the intersections of the ordinary with the fantasy realms of the unexplained. He uses language and word pictures vividly; his texts are more than mere popular novels. He has messages to share that transcend the "X-File-ish" universe he chooses to embody. He is one of many authors, contemporary or past, who captures and takes readers—and nonobserving audience members—to the arena of performed literature. Choose texts by authors who write vividly if you want texts to stand out in performance. One such other writer who uses vivid language and colorful word pictures is science fiction author Ray Bradbury.

2. ***Does the text have compelling characters?***: Another term for character is *persona*, the "voice" for ideas, conflicts, emotions, and insights. A persona could have a name or be an unknown yet embodied "spirit" to a text. Odd Thomas, in the previous selection, is a twenty-year-old short-order cook who has a "second sight ability" to see dead people before and after their demise. He is quirky, yet not portrayed as insane. He chooses to offer his abilities to local law enforcement and does so even when the minions of evil confront him and his friends. Since it is a "group" performance, do not select texts that exclusively focus on one persona. Even though *Odd Thomas* as a novel is told from the first-person point of view, it has elements that are not always centered on one person speaking. Choose texts with intriguing and dimensional character interaction, both verbal and nonverbal.

3. ***Does the text have definitive action?***: Psychological and emotional action work better for Readers Theatre than excessive physical action. Psychological closure works with mimed action to suggest physicality, but extensive physical action (e.g., fist fights or domestic violence rampages) without language accompaniment loses credibility. The scene of recognition in William Gibson's *The Miracle Worker* consists of a gripping, knock-down drag-out physical ordeal between Annie Sullivan and Helen Keller. However, eight minutes of mime actions, followed by the exultant cry, "Wah-, wah!" does not work well in Readers Theatre. Look for definitive, yet internalized action moments in texts you choose for Readers Theatre performance.

4. ***Is there a sense of wholeness, even within an episode or an edited portion of a larger work?***: An audience may not know a context for an edited portion of a text unless you provide it. It should be clear that a text has a beginning, a middle, and an end. Even if the text has been condensed, each portion should have wholeness qualities.

5. *Does the text have important messages to share?*: Look for texts that make comments on life or perspectives on our human choices as we exist. Gravitate to texts that express ideas that are provocative and novel, even profound. Look for "freshness" and unpredictability in texts that share rhetorical viewpoints on issues and concerns.

6. *Will the text have an appeal to your anticipated audience?*: Audiences like to experience ranges of feelings: humorous to sobering. Audiences respond better to texts that have been chosen for their timeliness or timelessness. Texts need not all be contemporary or recently popular to be appreciated by modern audiences. Choose texts that allow audiences to use their imaginations as part of the performance experience.

7. *Does the text fit an allocated time period?*: You may be limited by time, yet you want the text to be presented in enough of its entirety to adequately share its perspective. Edit in such a manner that important details are stated and provided.

8. *Can you cast it?*: Even though cast members can perform multiple roles, a performer should not present a multiple role interaction in a scene with oneself. A solo interpreter can and often does offer multiple personae in dialogue, but within a group performance the expectation exists that a performer will interact with another performer uniquely, one at a time. Most Readers Theatre performances average three to eight performers. Choose material that can be performed by the available cast numbers.

9. *If the text is not considered in the public domain, can you secure the rights to produce it?*: For educational classroom settings the presentation of copyrighted materials does not need royalty payments or publisher permissions. Forensics or festival presentations, usually offered without ticket purchases, are exempt as well in most cases, since they are extensions of

the educational setting in a classroom. If you charge admission for a presentation, royalty and permission payments are necessary for many dramatic texts, even excerpts performed, and the permissions are not always automatically granted. Public domain refers to literary texts that are usually more than seventy-five to one hundred years old and are not owned outright by any particular agency. The fair use and performing options for nondramatic literature are much more lenient than if you attempt to charge for a performance of a play, even one adapted to Readers Theatre. Check out the royalty information data inside the cover of plays if you are in doubt. The United States Copyright Office in Washington, D.C., publishes a fact sheet on fair use and permissions as well. Certainly selections from Shakespeare, the Bible, and many deceased authors, poets, and playwrights do not require permission nor payments for performance purposes. Most literary and nonliterary texts that you might use for performance may only require a citation reference, much like a footnote (e.g., newspaper editorials, journal entries, oral histories).

10. *Can the material be adapted so as to retain a writer's imprint, respecting his/her rights as original author?*: Even though, as we learned in Chapter 2, intertextuality concepts may blur an author's intent, there is a need to be faithful to the writer's original source. You should not alter the ending or the resolution to a text's plotline with additional lines or characters that never existed in the original text. All adaptors must be committed to the integrity of the original source. Juxtapose other lines to contrast an original text, but attempt to keep a semblance of an author's composition apparent in the adaptation process. Intertextuality should not be a license to provide "death to authorship." Transitional lines that are minimal can be added to assist the performable flow of a script, but never at the expense of drastic alterations in author-created elements.

Structure for Text Selection

Rarely do you begin the Readers Theatre production concept with a completed sense of message text placement. In most cases you begin with what Michael Leigh calls "free association":

> Free association is the crucible of most creativity. One sees two or more things not previously seen in connection with each other and one draws them together.... Most don't trust that unconscious process which is the beginning of all creations, the void from which there is light.[2]

Begin to collect literary texts and place them in file folders for later reference. While you obviously must begin with a text you liked for some reason, you must begin to link that "liked" story to source materials that connect to an important message for you and potential audiences. The "free association process" should happen as you visit these text files and ask yourself, "What message in these texts made me like them in the first place and now that I am re-reading them?" You are beginning the journey to select texts centered around a topic of real-world consequences.

Single Text Productions

In the single-text format one literary or oral tradition text comprises the entire production. Plays are the easiest single-format text to convert to Readers Theatre because they were originally written to be performed. Plays already have the lines divided between characters and an adaptor/director knows about how long the text will take to perform. One of the first professionally successful Readers Theatre productions on Broadway (see Chapter 1) was George Bernard Shaw's *Don Juan in Hell*, a middle act from the longer play, *Man and Superman*.

Plays that are language driven more than action driven translate well to Readers Theatre. Many Shakespearean plays have difficult literal staging qualities, but work well when the language use become the focus, while the action becomes imagined. A great RT option, the two-person play, *Love Letters* by A. L. Gurney, emphasizes the interaction through the mail more than physicalized action.

If a nondramatic piece of literature is chosen for production, the adaptor must divide up the text in bits and pieces of dialogue and description so that many voices speak or perform toward the one goal of the individual text. The text will probably require editing as well if a time or cast limit has been imposed. Long epic poems (e.g., Stephen Vincent Benét's *John Brown's Body*) or novels (e.g., Stephen King's *The Green Mile*) can be edited and adapted for performance. Many audiences are prepared for these nondramatic performances due in large part to the growth of "books on tape" or "CD versions of novels" that accompany the initial publication of popular novels (e.g., the Harry Potter books read by Jim Dale). A special kind of Readers Theatre focuses on one narrative fiction text and it is called *Chamber Theatre*. (More will be said about Chamber Theatre in Chapter 5.)

Compiled Text Formats

Compiled text formats frequently mix literary genres and build their presentations by juxtaposing and alternating pieces of literature. The compiled script may be an *expanded program* or a *collage* (see pages 42-43). Both formats can explore a theme, an argument, the works of an author, a historical period, or a literary genre/oral tradition.

Sometimes, but not always, that first text you found becomes a center "spoke" for you to explore and discover other texts that branch out from it. (See Figure 3.1.) But whatever text evolves into the center of your production, the other texts will find their working place. Like a compelling speech, effective Readers Theatre production scripts follow patterns. The *argument toward a conclusion* approach places a text in an order that ultimately wants the concluding text to the best

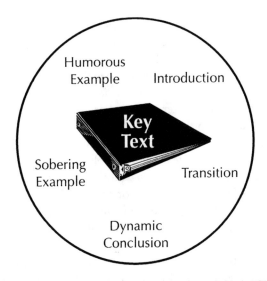

Relationship to Text in Compiled Scripts

Figure 3.1

"textual" evidence for believing an argument. The *symphonic structure* (e.g., ABCA) may introduce a main theme (A), hint at it again in the unique middle sections (B and C "movements"), and return to it in the conclusion (A). Some compiled programs explore a message or ideas expressed in the *past, present,* and *future.* A format could place texts by: *least to most important, causes/effects, comparison/contrast,* or *archetypes* (e.g., birth to death, coming of age, rituals, love, light to dark).

Collage-compiled scripts divide texts into smaller units, creating a new "whole." As in art, textual fragments are cut and pasted together to form a new entity. These fragments are scripted seamlessly by the adaptor, including scripted introductions and transitions. The collage script downplays the individual author of a text to create a new *source* for message intent—the adaptor. An adaptor could begin with a song lyric—sung or rhythmically spoken, segue to an original introduction, offer a stanza from a poem, segue by means of an original transition to two oral histories with alternating narrative connections, segue by transition to lines from a play, a newspaper editorial, or even an Internet blog and so forth until a concluding piece wraps up the scraps into a compelling argument and completed presentation.

Collage scripts seem to call for more original work from an adaptor. The greatest challenge for the adaptor in collage work is to use and honor individual authors' works, yet create a new holistic performance piece. This format frequently requires tinkering, additions, subtractions, excerpting, and rewriting even well into the rehearsal process.

On occasion a key literary selection may even create a seamless structure for the adaptor. In a compiled script with collage elements, I linked various selections together as examples of low-level to high-level stress moments as indicated on a psychological test for stress. "The Stress Mess" was a humorous program that progressed to more sobering concerns as the higher levels of stress took on tragic perspectives. Literary and oral tradition selections ranged from eating habits to the devastation of the death of a child or a spouse—all given increasing points toward a high stress personal score by the key journal article by the psychologists.

Each format has its own strengths and weaknesses. Single-text format allows for close analysis of a single mind's approach to message. Compiled scripts use a variety of literature to explore a theme or argument. Collage scripts break down individual texts to synergize into a new adaptor-centered art form. Some formats retain author perspective; others downplay and blur individual author contributions. Some formats develop complexities of a few personae; others call for range of characterizations to explore thematic connections. No matter the format, however, an adaptor/director must analyze and understand literary choices so as to help performers complete the communication through performance process.

Analyzing the Text: The Rhetorical/Argumentative Approach

In keeping with the communication process focus of this text, performers should prepare a *rhetorical/argumentative* approach to textual analysis. As you learned in Chapter 2 it certainly is not the only critical means to analyze a text. However, Yordon indicates that this approach "is concerned with the persuasive/communicative strategies within the literary work and with the effect the work has on its audience/readers."[3]

How can you embrace a *rhetorical/argumentative* approach to analysis, yet be committed to letting each text communicate on its own in a given context? At a basic level, the critic must create choices based on what can be ascertained about a text—its *certainties*. Personae in texts are frequently identifiable as male or female. Poetry that follows a particular formula is certain (e.g., the sonnet). Verb tense tells you if a story is past or present or future. From certainties, a critic can generate choices that may be *probable* or *possible*. Once the certainties are embraced and affirmed, the probabilities and possibilities lead the way toward creativity for the adaptor/director and performers alike.[4]

The rhetorical/argumentative approach will assist the adaptor/director to: (1) initially discover the primary ideas in a text, (2) develop an understanding of character decisions, (3) the role of imagery in a text, (4) elements of time, and (5) plot structure.

Primary Ideas in a Text

If you choose to produce a single text as a Readers Theatre production, you may find that its episodic nature introduces several themes. Still, one overarching theme, thesis, communicative statement, or argument should emerge. You may have to assist the audience by drawing attention to it in performance choices or original introductions and transitions.

If you choose to produce a compiled or collage script with many texts, you may need to decide which text best represents the primary idea for performance. (See Figure 3.1.) Its placement is crucial. Primacy and recency notions remind us that people tend to remember what they heard first as well as what they finally recall at the end of any program. Placing the most important text in a compiled script in the middle of multiple texts may result in confusion or the natural tendency to overlook it. Key texts in compiled scripts should be placed first or at the conclusion of a program.

Ideas also center around the *tone* or *attitude* of a text. Humorous portions of texts break dramatic tensions at times, but if the primary communicative message is serious, then ending a serious program with humor may minimize that serious impact.

Regardless of the performance format, some ideas in oral and literary texts seem to be contradictory. This juxtaposition of opposing ideas—the *paradox*—can add vitality to a production. Texts may reveal paradoxes in character traits or descriptive imagery or decision-making dilemmas. A program without some sort of conflict would be dull indeed.

Another characteristic to look for in ideas is the notion of *irony*. Irony is a specialized form of humor that may lead to sarcasm or thought-provoking "ah-ha!" moments of recognition. Irony is present when there is an apparent contradiction between the shared meaning of an idea and the actual language form the idea assumes.

Ideas in texts are rarely "telegraphed" or made painfully obvious. The power of an idea appears to be generated by context and implication more than direct statement. Implied ideas play powerfully in the Readers Theatre art form as they call forth demands for using one's active imagination as an observer.

At the outset of your analytical study of texts ask yourself, "What does this text say about a topic?" You may follow a process similar to arriving at a thesis for a speech. Your initial answer to the question will be broad, nonspecific, and rather generic. Say, for example, you determine the text(s) to be centered on the topic of love. You will need to refine your topic of *love* to a narrower, but less amorphous thesis. So love can be explored in texts that concentrate on unrequited love, first love, obsessive love, forbidden love, or unconditional love. Once you have determined a narrower focus, you should write out a complete sentence that expresses this summarized tone and thesis. That sentence may come from a text itself or be created by an adaptor and used in original introductions or transitions.

Consider the following poem:

To an Athlete Dying Young
By A. E. Housman (1859–1936)

The time you won your town the race
We chaired you through the market-place;
Man and boy stood cheering by,
And home we brought you shoulder-high.

To-day, the road all runners come,
Shoulder-high we bring you home,
And set you at your threshold down,
Townsman of a stiller town.

Smart lad, to slip betimes away
From fields where glory does not stay
And early though the laurel grows
It withers quicker than the rose.

Eyes the shady night has shut
Cannot see the record cut,
And silence sounds no worse than cheers
After earth has stopped the ears:

Now you will not swell the rout
Of lads that wore their honours out,
Runners whom renown outran
And the name died before the man.
So set, before its echoes fade,
The fleet foot on the sill of shade,
And hold to the low lintel up
The still-defended challenge-cup.

And round that early-laurelled head
Will flock to gaze the strengthless dead,
And find unwithered on its curls
The garland briefer than a girl's.

"To the Athlete Dying Young" from "A Shropshire Lad" – Authorised edition from
The Collected Poems of A.E. Houseman. Copyright 1939, 1940, 1965 by Henry Holt
and Company, copyright 1967, 1968 by Robert E. Symons. Reprinted by permission of
Henry Holt and Company, LLC.

What is this poem about? The title tells you some part of a central idea, but not its tone nor its perspective. Did you think about high school or college athletes who die prematurely? Did you think about young athletes who die in nonathletic endeavors (e.g., war)? How might this poem's central idea fit in with other textual contexts?

Analysis of Characters

In a single production text, a performer may be cast to represent one primary persona or one persona plus a few minor characters. Commitment to analysis of character can be focused and developed when the task centers on one text alone.

In a compiled production script, a performer will need to study each individual persona, perhaps finding a common thread for interpretation that embodies intertextuality. The brevity of textual development may require that you perform with a commitment to "back story" you may know (from the excerpt's context) or created to motivate performance choices.

A performer in a play or dramatized novel may have cues from an author who has explicitly created a persona. But where should a performer go to discover history, appearance, context, and experience when the persona is a third-person narrator or nondescript "voice" for a poem? The answer lies in choices generated by "character analysis." Look for examples of tone, attitude, notions of power or powerlessness, or psychological reactions. Some personae are forthright; others are secretive or shy. Some personae are overtly emotional; others are like tea kettles ready to explode with "steam" (anger) at any second.

You may find it helpful to create a "back story" for a character, aspects of life never mentioned but internalized by a performer to motivate actual textual lines. Characters find their individualized power through interior thinking, ranges of emotional expression, and their vitality and energy.

You may have experience as a performer playing a character part in conventional theatre. But you may have never considered that preparing to perform the part of a narrator may be equally as provocative and challenging. Narrators generate interest by virtue of their perspectives and control over the contexts they describe. You must come to know narrators and lyric poetry personae as fully as you would know an embodied and named character.

Sensory Imagery in Texts

Gifted authors know how to use language to create word pictures and the Readers Theatre performer becomes the conduit to place that imagery in the minds of a listening audience. Texts rich in imagery appeal to our human senses as well as the cognitive ability to make connections mentally so as to enhance the imagined vision.

Two unlike objects that are identified by direct comparison use the figure of speech known as *metaphor* (e.g., "He was a low-down, snake-in-the-grass."). *Simile* compares attributes of dissimilar objects with words such as "like" or "as" (e.g., "She had a face like an angel's.").

A performer must understand the imagery used in so many other figures of speech as they appear in a given text even to a greater extent than does a member of a listening audience. Besides the previously mentioned linguistic uses of imagery, a performer must study and analyze aspects of seven primary sensory details:

1. *Auditory Imagery:* Sounds of words create images. Words with inherent "sounds" are said to have *onomatopoeia* (e.g., "buzz, clang, whirr, gurgle, etc.").

2. *Visual Imagery:* Usually driven by adjectives connected to objectified nouns, descriptions that evoke "scenes" in our minds gain power in performance. "Purple mountains' majesty above the fruited plain" creates a vast spectacle of open places dominated by nature's topography every time we sing or hear "America the Beautiful".

3. *Kinetic and Kinesthetic Imagery:* Kinetic details describe physical action, while kinesthetic imagery suggests the physical action or anxiety levels we sense within our bodies. Kinetic imagery describes external action; kinesthetic imagery describes feelings of activity we have internally. Consider the plight of Dr. Watson, seeing the mountain climbing gear of his friend Sherlock Holmes left at the precipice of the Reichenbach Falls, and the rush of emotions that gush forth from the obvious implications:

49

"The Final Problem"
by Sir Arthur Conan Doyle

In a tingle of fear I was already running down the village street, and making for the path which I had so lately descended. It had taken me an hour to come down. For all my efforts, two more had passed before I found myself at the fall of Reichenbach once more. There was Holmes's alpenstock still leaning against the rock by which I had left him. But there was no sign of him, and it was in vain that I shouted. My only answer was my own voice reverberating in a rolling echo from the cliffs around me.

It was the sight of that alpenstock which turned me cold and sick....He had remained on that three-foot path, with sheer wall on one side and sheer drop upon the other, until his enemy had overtaken him....

I stood for a minute or two to collect myself, for I was dazed with the horror of the thing. Then I began to think of Holmes's own methods and to try to practice them in reading this tragedy. It was, alas! only too easy to do. During our conversation we had not gone to the end of the path, and the alpenstock marked the place where we had stood. The blackish soil is kept forever soft by the incessant drift of spray, and a bird would leave its tread upon it. Two lines of footmarks were clearly marked along the further end of the path, both leading away from me. There were none returning. A few yards from the end the soil was all ploughed up into a patch of mud, and the brambles and ferns which fringed the chasm were torn and bedraggled. I lay upon my face and peered over, with the spray spouting up all around me. It had darkened since I had left, and now I could only see here and there the glistening of moisture upon the black walls, and far away down at the end of the shaft the gleam of the broken water. I shouted; but only that same half-human cry of the fall was borne back to my ears.

But it was destined that I should after all have a last word of greeting from my friend and comrade. I have said that

50

his alpenstock had been left leaning against a rock which jutted on to the path. From the top of this boulder the gleam of something bright caught my eye, an, raising my hand, I found that it came from the silver cigarette case which he used to carry. As I took it up a small square of paper upon which it had lain fluttered down on to the ground. Unfolding it I found that it consisted of three pages torn from his notebook and addressed to me. It was characteristic of the man that the direction was as precise, and the writing as firm and clear, as though it had been written in his study.

"MY DEAR WATSON," he said, "I write these few lines through the courtesy of Mr. Moriarty, who awaits my convenience for the final discussion of those questions which lie between us. He has been giving me a sketch of the methods by which he avoided the English police and kept himself informed of our movements. They certainly confirm the very high opinion which I had formed of his abilities. I am pleased to think that I shall be able to free society from any further effects of his presence, though I fear that it is at a cost which will give pain to my friends, and especially, my dear Watson, to you. I have already explained to you, however, that my career had in any case reached its crisis, and that no possible conclusion to it could be more congenial to me than this. Indeed, if I may make a full confession to you, I was convinced that the letter from Meiringen was a hoax, and I allowed you to depart on that errand under the persuasion that some development of this sort would follow. Tell Inspector Patterson that the papers which he needs to convict the gang are in pigeonhole M, done up in a blue envelope and inscribed 'Moriarty.' I made every disposition of my property before leaving England, and handed it to my brother Mycroft. Pray give my greetings to Mrs. Watson, and believe me to be, my dear fellow,
    "Very sincerely yours,
    'SHERLOCK HOLMES.'"

A few words may suffice to tell the little that remains. An examination by experts leaves little doubt that a personal contest between the two men ended, as it could hardly fail to end in such a situation, in their reeling over, locked in each other's arms. Any attempt at recovering the bodies was absolutely hopeless, and there, deep down in that dreadful cauldron of swirling water and seething foam, will lie for all time the most dangerous criminal and the foremost champion of the law of their generation....As to the gang, it will be within the memory of the public how completely the evidence which Holmes had accumulated exposed their organisation, and how heavily the hand of the dead man weighed upon them. Of their terrible chief few details came out during the proceeding, and if I have now been compelled to make a clear statement of his career, it is due to those injudicious champions who have endeavoured to clear his memory by attacks upon him whom I shall ever regard as the best and wisest man whom I have ever known.

[Source: from Sir Arthur Conan Doyle, *The Memoirs of Sherlock Holmes* (©1893 A. Conan Doyle) New York: Harper & Brothers, 1894)]

What kinetic and kinesthetic imagery does Conan Doyle use to evoke a terror that a close friend has plummeted to his death? What is there about the imagery used by Conan Doyle that makes this excerpt from his short story so "emotional"?

4. *Tactile data:* Language choices frequently rely on sensations generated by descriptions of touching behaviors. "He couldn't let well enough alone; he had to touch the burning embers in the seemingly dormant fireplace" is the cry of mothers trying to teach their young children to avoid unnecessary pain. Can you find any uses of tactile imagery in the previously mentioned Conan Doyle story?

5. *Gustatory imagery*: When we experience enjoyable or repulsive tastes, we use gustatory senses. Imagery to describe the taste of your favorite meal will use different language than words used to describe a cold medicine with an ingredient with a bitter aftertaste.

6. *Olfactory impressions*: When we recall strong scents and the smells bring satisfaction or nausea, we use our olfactory senses. Children can recall the distinct smell of "grandmothers." Marijuana is not easily masked, but easily sniffed in the air when someone nearby is smoking it.

7. *Thermal reactions*: When we recall feeling hot or cold and accompanying body reactions (e.g., sweating or "shivers"), we use our thermal senses. Can you find some examples of thermal reactions in the Conan Doyle short story as well?

Were you saddened at all by the Conan Doyle short story? Did it remind you of a frightening experience of your own? The personal associations that we all experience come to be matched when we analyze texts for performance. It is as if we reexperience or even vicariously experience sensations that we can not only read about, but now perform as well. The analytical experience implants the performed text in the arena of our minds first. Our minds allow us to encounter hundreds of locales, sensations, feelings, memories, and ultimately new messages as well.

Elements of Time

Not all texts follow linear progression. Some events may be relayed in flashbacks, revealing occurrences at an earlier time. Some texts take detours or have intentional digression from a primary idea. Analysis will generate choices to perform as if time is slowing (slow motion) or rapidly increasing (sped up to incoherent babbling). Pausing or timely silences can stop time or portend something ominous to come when time resumes its normal unfolding.

I am going to ask you to take another look at both the A. E. Housman poem as well as the Arthur Conan Doyle short story once again and determine how variations in pacing (slow to fast) and pausing with silence offers up the sensation of time itself. Why did you decide to slow down or speed up? What difference does it make if you pause? Does it alter any other sensations than that of time?

Plot Structure in Analysis

All texts that generate responsiveness have sequences of plot structure that relate to each other. Four aspects of this structure should be analyzed and understood: *build, crisis, climax,* and *denouement.*

The build consists of introductory action elements found in a text before the climax. From the first word, the build should have aspects that increase the fervor and the intensity of an unfolding story line. The build need not be quick or feel rushed; a build can be subtle and methodical, but obvious and noticeable. Creating or understanding a sense of build does not occur because a group of performers read faster or perform with louder volume. Frequently, a build includes expositional introductions of characters, context, and tone. A play, for example, usually has much more exposition in the beginning of Act One than later on in the play. An adaptor/director as well as the performer must analyze a text and decide when and how the intensity levels of the build should surpass each previous level or "point" toward a climax. If a build is not sensed or planned, the performance seems static and ultimately lulling. The worst sin to commit in a group performance is to bore an audience by insensitivities to aspects of the build.

Complex texts or compiled script texts have a moment in the build wherein the plot or the tone changes direction and the primary idea emerges. Crisis sets up a logical progression of factors that originate with this element. Performers need to emphasize the crisis sensitively but obviously. An adaptor/director who positions excerpts or juxtaposed texts will need to know how alterations in tone or changes in texts move the performance toward the crisis.

When a crisis hits a peak level of intensity or emotionality, a climax emerges. Characterized by fervor and emotionalism, the climax calls forth performers' full arsenal of presentational skills. A climax has minimal impact if performers fail to build and point to a crisis. Sudden, unmotivated outbursts without logical, progressive performance choices make a climax seem like a surprise or a melodramatic exercise. The serious peak moment can be embarrassing or dismissed by an ill-prepared audience.

Sometimes you will notice during your own personal analysis that the climax of the performance script occurs at the end of the final selection. But this is not required nor true for all single or compiled text scripts.

The intensity level of a climax usually requires a gradual decreasing before a text concludes. Referred to as the denouement, or falling action, this sequence calls on performers to decrease intensity and gradually stop. In some cases, the denouement may be as short as a phrase or sentence. Collage scripts sometimes script a technique for the denouement known as *summary particles*. Portions of lines from previous text samples, rapidly delivered, slowing to a gradual halt, remind the audience of key textual elements in this method. More frequently, a scripted text adds paragraphs or stanzas to wrap up action. Performers who choose to make the final line of a scripted text serve as climax may use silence to impart a sensation of denouement before departing the performing area. Performers dare not dismiss the power of denouement. You steal an important moment of resolution and completeness for an audience when you rush a climax, hurriedly exit the scene, and do not let the final moment hover in closure for the performers as well as the audience.

<u>Conclusion</u>

Now you may be saying to yourself, "All this analysis seems like I'm dissecting a frog in biology. I have torn apart the literature and I can't possibly see how it all fits back together." To further the analogy, however, performers cannot truly understand the interactions of structure, character, audience, and textual language by observing the whole text ("frog") or even merely trying to duplicate the prescriptive dictates of the adaptor/director. Good adaptors/directors need to have a sense of analysis, but be open to discussions with their casts of differing choices for performances. Once all has been laid out on the "table," however, the adaptor/director makes the ultimate choices and performers should attempt to match those perspectives. You must "cut away," label, identify, contemplate, learn — the individual components of a whole. You do this so that as the parts are presented, the message of the whole is clear and consistent and dimensional.

Why is analysis necessary? It provides the performers of literature with critical choices useful in communicating the message of the chosen texts. "It is the responsibility of the performer to make critical choices to determine the best way to communicate the message. The performance of the literature is the means by which the message is conveyed."[5] Analysis ultimately ensures that both the adaptor/director and performers will remain as true to the integrity of a text as is possible. According to John Creagh, "performers do more than embody the printed page; they allow the others in the text to inhabit their physical selves, making performance a rich synthesis of text and performer."[6] And analysis of texts for performance has a residual benefit too. Researchers have found that the strategies and techniques used by professional actors when they must memorize large quantities of lines for a performance begin with analytical study, character motivation, and the kind of background study described in this chapter. You may or may not be required to memorize your scripts for classroom performances, but you will certainly be expected to be familiar with what the script communicates. The findings of the current research remind us that textual analysis is so important because "memory is tremendously dependent on context…and creating a context [through analysis] for what we need to remember can go a long way to lock that word, or fact, or list, or name, into our minds….If you haven't focused on the meaning of the message, you won't remember it very well."[7]

Discussion and Assignments

1. Choose some class members (3–5) to read from a binder or
    present a memorized version of any of the three literary
    excerpts found in this chapter. For everyone else in class, bring
    a literary or oral textual selection to class next session and be
    prepared to read from a binder or perform from memory that
    selection. Choose an excerpt or a complete text that is 3 to 5
    minutes in length. This will provide an opportunity for assess-
    ing skill testing as well as provide an opportunity to answer
    analytical questions, such as:

    (a) Does the performer make compelling presentational
        choices? Why? Why not?

    (b) Does the performer understand the language of the text?

    (c) Does the persona or personae *change*, *evolve*, or *develop*
        during this short presentation?

    (d) Is (Are) the persona(e) credible?

    (e) Can you sense a build, a crisis, a climax, or a denouement
        in this brief selection?

    (f) Does the performer help me understand the primary idea,
        see imagery, sense changes in time, and gain a sense of
        plot structure?

2. Take another look at the brief Dean Koontz portion, the A. E.
    Houseman poem, and the Conan Doyle short story excerpt
    and indicate whether or not you think any of these texts could
    be adapted for group performance. Most of the lines relate to
    one persona. How can dividing up the lines between more than
    one person help share a text's primary idea? In the Appendix,

use the excerpt from the Conan Doyle short story as an exercise in dividing up the lines.

3. Do you agree with the psychological studies that memory can be enhanced and made easier if context is understood prior to rote memory tasks? What has been your own experience as you have memorized lines for plays? How do you go about this task? When does it become easier?

References

1. Beverly Whitaker Long, Lee Hudson, and Phillis Rienstra Jeffrey, *Group Performance of Literature* (Englewood Cliffs, NJ: Prentice-Hall, Inc., 1977), 6.

2. Michael G. Leigh, *The Care and Feeding of Readers Theatre: A Manual for Instructors and Directors* (Privately published and copyrighted by Michael G. Leigh: 1991), 27.

3. Judy E. Yordon, *Roles in Interpretation*—5th Edition. (Boston: McGraw-Hill, 2002), 85.

4. See: Long, Hudson, Jeffrey, *Group Performance of Literature*, 17–18.

5. Liana B. Koeppel and Mark T. Morman, "Oral Interpretation Events and Argument: Forensics Discourse or Aesthetic Entertainment?" *National Forensic Journal*, 9 (Fall 1991), 146.

6. John Creagh, "The Interpersonal Metaphor in Literary Criticism: Towards An Attribution-Based Model of Literary Response," *The Carolinas Speech Communication Annual*, 2 (1986), 22.

7. Marianne Szegedy-Maszak, "Memory Takes a Cue from Acting," *Los Angeles Times* (Health; Section F: February 20, 2006): F1, F10.

4

Performance Choices

Since you are enrolled in this group performance course, the assumption is that you have completed a previous course in oral interpretation or solo performance of literature or basic acting. Much of the previous course focused on learning basic performance skills. Thus, in this chapter we will concentrate on a review of performance choices for the individual performer who works with fellow performers in group presentations.

I have chosen to divide the next two segments into parts in order to facilitate the discussion. But the truth is, however, that "it is impossible to study either verbal or nonverbal communication as isolated structures. Rather, these systems should be regarded as a unified communication construct."[1] A review for understanding of this construct will help performers hone their skills and adaptors/directors offer suggestions for motivated and exceptional presentations.

Nonverbal Performance Choices

Nonverbal communication is the study of body language, facial expressions, physical appearance and clothing choices, space, territory, touching behaviors, time, and the environment. (This chapter will focus on all these aspects except for environment, which shares nonverbal messages by architecture or symbols and will be revisited in Chapter 7 on design and staging concepts.) In performance, nonverbal responses seem to be fluid in that once offered one learns to live, adapt, or adjust with the consequences.

Nonverbal communication can serve two functions: (1) *reinforcement* or support for a verbal message, or (2) a *separate* communication immune to any linguistic alternative interpretation that stands alone. When the appearance of message intent is *mixed* or *contradictory*, nonverbal communication can reveal a secretive or "hidden agenda."

Assuming that a performer has made some analytical choices, the presentation must reveal consistent nonverbal choices with that analysis. A text that calls for anger brings forth body tensions to reinforce the angry tone. If mixed or contradictory messages occur, the nonverbal aspects tend to be believed first. Actions do indeed speak louder than words.

Of the hundreds of behaviors, objects, and events identified as examples of nonverbal communication, all have the potential to communicate meaning to an audience. To aid the performers of literature these examples are divided into the following classifications: kinesics, oculesics, physical appearance and clothing choices, proxemics, haptics, and chronemics.

Kinesics

Kinesics refers to the study of body movement, gestures, and posture. Carefully chosen body movements greatly aid the performer of literature. Some hand gestures are culture bound and have a specific meaning. These gestures that fully substitute for spoken words are called *emblems*. Emblems vary with culture and some emblems are acceptable in one culture, but interpreted as obscene or confrontational in others. The circular "sign" for "A-OK" (thumb connected with middle finger) intends encouragement and support in some cultures, but an obscenity in others. *Illustrator* gestures help reinforce and clarify speech by accompanying verbal statements. Performers use the illustrators to share nuances in a text or believable personae. They can also function as nonverbal means to conceptualize possible confusing descriptions (e.g., both hands to show size and shape of a box) or even "underline" with a jabbing hand gesture, suggesting the importance of a concept.

Two other kinesic behaviors assist any performer in assessing how a performance is being perceived. *Regulator* responses consist of head nods in affirmation or negation, hand gestures that indicate connection or rejection, or posture shifts to suggest interest or boredom. In a group performance, regulators are usually offered when another performer speaks. *Affect displays* are linked to facial expressions of emotions, posture attitude, and internalized physical tension.

A final example of kinesic behavior called *adaptors*. These gestures are merely frequent, revealing much about a character's internal state. While not usually communicating anything directly, adaptors may be any kind of "stage business" that uniquely defines a persona. For example, some poker players like to "play" with their chips, nervously separating and restacking their chips with one hand before offering a wager.

Oculesics

Any performer must know the range of his/her abilities to express communication with facial expressions and eye behavior. This study, known as *oculesics*, reveals how humans express interpersonal feelings, serve as regulators, show anxiety, tension, sadness, arousal, surprise, joy, and related behaviors. The face is the most communicative part of the body and one's eyes are the most communicative part of the face.

Performers learn quickly the power and impact of *eye gaze*. In simplest terms it means looking at another person or object. As we will discover later in the chapter, Readers Theatre performers are frequently called upon to simulate reciprocal eye-to-eye gaze by means of various focal points. What must never be acceptable is the perception of *eye glaze*, the vacant expressionless lack of discernment—unless, of course, the personal is blind or requires a nonconnected eye glaze simulation for some reason.

Physical Appearance and Clothing

A conventional theatre actor is frequently cast for a part based on physical appearance. As a presentational art form, Readers Theatre can suggest character by means other than precise physical appearance. Age, gender, body type, and beauty are not hindrances for any member of the group performance of literature. All these can be suggested nonverbally or vocally.

While Chamber Theatre presentations may demand precise costumes (see Chapter 5), other presentational group performances only require a sensitivity to color coding or ensemble dress. Colored turtleneck shirts, commonly colored slacks or jeans, or other ensemble appearance can link the group together. And small additions of clothing from a hat rack or set piece can subtly share a change in persona or mood within a performance piece.

An adaptor/director cannot merely say to a cast, "Wear whatever you like," because an audience may be set up to interpret clothing choices as part of the imaginative task of viewing. Do not underdress (too casual) or overdress (too formal). Wear colors and clothing that ultimately allows any text to be creatively imagined.

Proxemics and Haptics

The study of how we use personal space and territory is called *proxemics*. Since Readers Theatre relies on any found space, the proximity to an audience could be closer than the normal conventional theatre offering. Generally, the farther away you are from an audience, the more likely you are to communicate messages of distance, distrust, aloofness, coldness, and lack of empathy or friendliness. As you move closer to an audience, performers are psychologically perceived as more personal and genuine. However, if you invade the comfort zone of space and are too close to an audience, you signal intimidation, lack of sensitivity, domination, and combativeness. Find the comfortable range in your space and territory. Variations in backing up or stepping forward keep an audience interested in your presentation.

You may or may not actually touch other performers in a Readers Theatre. Sometimes the imagination is allowed to run free if touching behaviors are simulated or mimed. Called *haptics* or *tactile communication*, touching shares a range of feelings, both attractive and repulsive.

Using proxemics and haptics creates opportunities for all performers to achieve that rare moment when they have the listeners "right in the palm of the hand," a feeling of empathy and interrelatedness that is thrilling when it occurs in any performance.

Chronemics

The study of how humans interpret structure and make use of their time is called *chronemics*. Pacing and pausing are crucial elements involving time in any group performance. Perform too fast/too often and audiences feel rushed and bewildered. Pause too long and audiences may think you forgot a line. Have a silence be too long and without responsiveness an audience experiences a lull in attention.

If you are constrained by a time limit, the performance needs to be close to the expected completion time. On the other hand, a performance that seems too brief may call forth an audience response of demanding more for their "buck" or time spent watching.

Nonverbally, you may simulate time progressing, speeding up, going into slow motion, or "freezing" by variations in physicality. And, if you are simulating a telephone conversation, you will need to pause ever so slightly after each response to act as if you are listening or receiving a response to your previous comment. Avoid missing subtextual calls for sensitivity to issues of time while you perform.

Vocal Performance Choices

The bridge that brings nonverbal forms and vocal factors together is called *paralanguage*. Paralanguage is not what you say (content) necessarily, but how you say it (feelings for the implication). By altering a range of vocal cues you can shade or provide a variety of meanings to virtually any spoken word or phrase. Consider these three categories for paralinguistic variables: voice qualities, vocal set, and vocalizations.

Voice Qualities

Vocal qualities function within ranges and they include pitch, volume, tempo and rhythm, articulation and pronunciation, and finally resonance. Each of these qualities makes use of the sound-making properties of the human voice.

Pitch refers to the range of highness to lowness in your voice. Changing pitches (*inflections*) reveals a variety of feeling and intent. Having your pitch trail off at the end of an idea or sentence suggests completion. Having your pitch end high in inflection turns any sentence into a question. Having your pitch go high and low within a complete idea or sentence (*circumflex pitch*) suggests sarcasm, disbelief, innuendo, or even "hidden agenda." Changes in pitch can also suggest age or gender differences. Choral line readings in Readers Theatre may require that some performers say lines at the upper portions or lower portions of the pitch range in order to create a harmonious "solo sounding" unified choral "voice."

The loudness to softness continuum constitutes *volume* levels. Volume has energy, emphasis, and focal force. The diaphragm, a muscle in the stomach region, generates this energy. When you "fill" an arena or found space with your voice, you direct your voice to a specific target. Projecting your voice can suggest distance or "calling out" to someone far away. In the opposite mode, stage whispers or asides still must be heard but the projection is more breathy and subdued. Feelings shared by volume changes include anger, alarm, and confrontation as volume levels increase and shyness, uncertainty, and nervousness become implied when volume levels decrease. Vocal force is the oral equivalent of underlining words or using italics; so as you punch the volume briefly on key words or phrases, you draw attention to important concepts.

The rate or pace of performance comprises the *tempo*. A dramatic piece may have much more plodding tempos than a comedy farce that works only if the tempo seems frenetic. We discussed the power of pausing as a component of chronemics, but pauses have an overlapping "verbal" role. Pausing may set up a joke line. Pausing helps tempo perception by signaling the end of a thought unit, providing time for an idea to sink in, and allowing the audience to know when the performer is at the logical end of the selection or performance.

Most texts have an inherent rhythm. In poetry the rhythms tend to be more apparent, but an adaptor/director can create rhythms in prose or dramatic literature often by the manner in which the line is divided among the performing group. Rhythm control in line delivery moves along a pattern such as from smooth to jerky to placid with strategically placed pauses or no pauses.

Two terms (articulation and pronunciation) are related, but not identical. *Articulation* (or *enunciation*) is the process of forming sounds, syllables, and words crisply and distinctly with the physical features that produce speech. *Pronunciation*, however, is knowing and speaking a word as it is correctly understood within a culture, subculture, or region. Poor articulation or mispronunciation is distracting and impacts listener perceptions.

To incorporate a regional or cultural dialect you may need to practice with taped exercises or pamphlet examples with pronunciation symbols. For example, not all British or American Southern dialects pronounce words in the same manner. You may need to incorporate *clipping* (chopping off syllables, letters, or sounds at the ends of words) or *drawling* (elongating vowel sounds and syllabic portions of words).

When air from your lungs vibrates the larynx ("voice box"), the resulting interaction causes *resonance* or *vocal timbre*. As the air vibrates the larynx, you can alter the sound by use of your teeth, tongue, and nasal cavity, shading tones and attitudes to the words you say aloud. Too much air that escapes through the larynx produces a "breathy" sound. Restricting the air crossing the vocal folds makes the voice sound "tense." Constricting your throat creates a "raspy" resonance. Too much resonance in the nasal passage creates a "nasal twang." Blocking resonation from the nasal cavity creates the sound of a person with a severe head cold. The "oratorical/preacher" sound occurs when you use too much resonance in the mouth cavity along with a loud, projected vocal quality.

Vocal Set

Some aspects of vocal qualities are linked to physical and psychological characteristics of human speech. A persona that stutters will have a vocal set that includes blocking on certain words and sounds as well as repetitive sounds that anticipate the desired word to be uttered.

A character that has a smoking problem will have a vocal set of coughing and wheezing while attempting to speak. Famous actors frequently study a character and provide them with a collection of vocal set distinctions. Dustin Hoffman reproduced the repetitive phraseology of an autistic man in the film, *Rain Man*. Meryl Streep has been rewarded with numerous Oscars and nominations for a wide range of characterizations. Philip Seymour Hoffman captured but did not caricature the quirky voice for author/celebrity Truman Capote in the film, *Capote*. These actors exemplify the wide range of possible vocal set usages for all performers of literature.

Vocalizations

Vocal sounds or noises may be understood as having meaning but separated from normal language. Billy Bob Thornton made his character recognizable to all with his guttural "Unh-hunh" responses to his internal thoughts in the independent film, *Sling Blade*. Other examples of vocalizations include *vocal characterizers* such as crying, laughing, whispering, belching, yawning, whining, and groaning. There are also *vocal emblems,* sounds that share meaning but do not have normal spelling usage (e.g., "Uh—huh" [affirmative]; "Hunh—uh" [negative]; "Sh—" [quiet]; "Ah—ah" [don't try it]; and "Hmmmm" [I wonder]. *Vocalized pauses* may or may not be scripted in a text but substitute for lack of anything else to say or mental unawareness (e.g., "OK," "Well," "And, uh," "You know," " Uh").

Choosing Focus

Once you have analyzed each text in a program, you must decide where you will place characters and scene action, as well as where eye gaze will find its location. *Focus* is the term used to describe the location of characters and scene action in various performed texts.

Focus in the group performance of literature can occur in four distinct ways: *audience focus, offstage focus, onstage focus,* and *inner-expressed focus.* Audience focus consists of direct eye contact between performers and listeners. It is usually the focus for narrative literature (prose) and occasionally drama (when the performer acknowledges the audience as onlookers). Poetry can use audience focus as can oral histories or ethnographies if the persona involved seems to be addressing a universal audience, not a particular person. Offstage focus suggests that another persona in a text is present or in dialogue. Eye gaze places this "imagined" persona slightly above the heads of the audience "suggesting" the existence of the other persona. Offstage focus may also be used

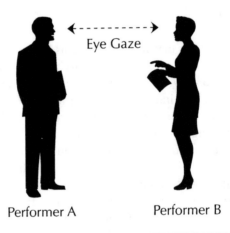

Eye Gaze

Performer A   Performer B

On-Stage Focus

Figure 4.1

to point out imagined scene components, inanimate objects, and progress when coupled with a narrative overlay of audience focus. Onstage focus is the focus of most conventional theatre. Actors look directly into the eyes of fellow actors who are adjacent to them. Readers Theatre productions may use onstage focus, but rarely does it dominate an entire program. Its use seems to signal intimacy or casual, yet

70

friendly relationships. Inner-expressed focus has no particular focal point, but is the outward expression of internalized thoughts. Inner-expressed focus is used for soliloquies or audible prayer or merely speaking what is on your mind.

Eye gaze determines where a scene is located. Offstage focal points may be "wedged" (seeing the "other" character at the apex), or cross-focused (speaking to someone but not actually seeing them; e.g. speaking through a door). Focus in a Readers Theatre production can be *mixed*,

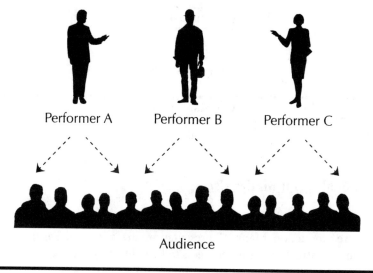

Figure 4.2

but it should never be *inconsistent*. It makes sense to mix in an omniscient narrator who can look onstage and at the audience, while two other performers only "see" the other with consistent offstage focus. It is distracting and misleading to have one performer address a persona offstage while the other performer responds by sneaking a look or glaring at the other performer onstage.

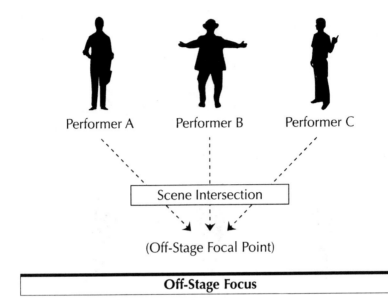

Performer A   Performer B   Performer C

Scene Intersection

(Off-Stage Focal Point)

Off-Stage Focus

Figure 4.3

Optional Script Binder Use

A three-ring binder no longer needs to be present to justify a Readers Theatre production. Many RT presentations are memorized as in traditional theatre. But if a notebook is to be used, there are conventions that can assist the performer.

The script that is perceived symbolically reminds an audience that a text is the focus, not necessarily a set, theatrical embellishments, or even a performer. A notebook can be transformed into a creative device or prop or any other suggested object or action.

What the notebook cannot become is a crutch to lean on. Its presence is not license for lack of preparation or concentration. The performance of literature will remain artistic expression with or without a script present, but if present you must look up and out of the notebook at least 60 percent of the time. If you choose to use a notebook, follow these guidelines:

1. Keep the script high enough to allow your eyes to lower to pick up the lines without bobbing your head up and down.

2. Do not allow the script to creep up so high that it blocks any portion of your face.

3. Hold the notebook in the same approximate position; raising and lowering the script without motivation is distracting.

4. Pick up the next line or phrase ahead of where you are reading to maintain longer intervals of eye gaze.

5. Even if the text is memorized, when a script is present, pages should be turned.

6. The 7 by 9 inch three-ring binder with a solid color cover is the easiest to use because it can be cradled by the spine in one hand. Flimsy cover term paper holders do not work well in Readers Theatre shows because they require continued two-handed maintenance.

7. Occasionally reference the text by looking down, even if it is memorized.

Conclusion

The remaining portion of this textbook now moves to a focus on how to adapt literature for group performance and create the production guide for the adaptor/director. Once the production guide and performance script are completed, you may want to return to these preliminary chapters to assist you in helping performers catch the vision for the production you have. Give suggestions for nonverbal and vocal uses. Watch where performers look and remind them of focal point consistency. Determine whether or not you will perform with notebook scripts.

All performance choices work successfully if the audience understands them. Wait for the audience to give you their attention before you begin. Slightly pause, but definitely, at the end of the performance, letting the last thought linger. And enjoy each moment of the group performance of literature process as you explore the communicative world of ideas awaiting you.

Discussion and Assignments

1. Review and practice using gestures as you say the following
    phrases and sentences:

    (a) He is this much taller than I am.

    (b) "Bring out your dead."—Monty Python and the Holy Grail

    (c) Stay away from me, you hear me?!

    (d) Please, come this way, sir.

    (e) Turn to the right up there at the next corner, please. Thanks.

    (f) You can put the dishes on the table right there.

    (g) Look, I'm telling you it won't work!

    (h) You can't really mean that?

    (i) What in the world are you doing?

    (j) Well, here I am. What do you want me to do now?

    (k) Hey, that's a great idea!

    (l) Well, it doesn't make any difference to me.

    (m) Don't get excited!!

    (n) Out! Do you hear me...out!

    (o) Come on, come on, come on. I don't have all day!

2. Read the following exercises out loud, utilizing various levels of vocal projection to suggest distance, close proximity, confidentiality, or desire to get someone's attention:

   (a) Mom, could you leave a house key before you head out? MOM, I need the house key!

   (b) OK, first thing is put the letters over there on the desk. JACK, could you go over to the theatre storage area and bring us back a step ladder? THANKS. Cheri, you want to follow Jack over there to be sure he gets that ladder. He may not know where it is.

   (c) Can you believe that dress she has on? I wouldn't be caught dead in something that tacky. OH, Jenny, Hi! Cute dress! Where'd you get it?

3. In the following exercise, read each line out loud, placing vocal force where necessary in order to emphasize the correct intent of the message. This is tricky, but give it a try:

   Ned Nott was shot and Sam Shott was not,
   So it's better to be Shott than Nott,
   Some say Nott was not shot, but Shott swears he shot Nott.
      Either the shot Shott shot at Nott was not shot or Nott
      was not shot.
   If the shot Shott shot shot Nott, Nott was shot,
      But if the shot Shott shot shot Shott himself, then Shott
      would be shot and Nott would not.
   However, the shot Shott shot shot not Shott but Nott.
   It's not easy to say who was shot and who was not,
   But we know what was Shott and who was Nott.[2]

76

4. For articulation practice, say the following tongue twisters three times each, saying each subsequent one faster than the previous time:

Six slim sleek saplings.
Old, oily Ollie oils oily autos.
The bottom of the butter bucket is the buttered bucket bottom.
Fill the sieve with thistles; then sift the thistles through the sieve.
She sells seashells, sherry and sandals on the seashore.
The beasts came to feast, but the geese had ceased and were to be released.

5. Make the proper pronunciation distinction between the following words and sentences that are identical yet different:

(a) We polish the Polish furniture.

(b) He could lead if he would get the lead out.

(c) A farm can produce produce.

(d) The soldier determined he would desert in the desert.

(e) The present is a good time to present the present.

(f) The buck does funny things when the does are present.

(g) After a number of Novocaine injections, my jaw got number.

(h) They sent a sewer down to stitch the tear in the sewer line.

6. If a text has no clear implied audience where would you determine to focus to be? Why?

7. Should you stare in offstage focus at the same location above the heads of the audience for long periods of time? Why or why not? When we give people direct eye contact, do we always stare in the same place for long periods of time?

8. Could a Readers Theatre program have some performers with notebooks and some without? Under what circumstances would this use of notebooks as scripts make sense?

Additional Reading

Andersen, Peter A. *Nonverbal Communication: Forms and Functions.* Mountain View, CA: Mayfield Publishing Company, 1999.

Knapp, Mark L. and Hall, Judith A. *Nonverbal Communication in Human Interactions.* Belmont, CA: Wadsworth Publishing Company, 2001.

Rizzo, Raymond. *The Voice As An Instrument*—2nd Edition. Indianapolis: Bobbs—Merrill Educational Publishing, 1978.

Sprague, Jo, and Stuart, Douglas. *The Speaker's Handbook*—6th Edition. Belmont, CA: Wadsworth/Thomson Learning Inc., 2003.

Stern, David Alan. *Acting with an Accent.* Los Angeles: Dialect Accent Specialists, Inc., 1979.

References

1. D. J. Higginbotham and D. E. Yoder, "Communication within Natural Conversational Interaction: Implications for Severe Communicatively Impaired Persons," *Topics in Language Disorders*, 2 (1982), 4.

2. Roger Karshner, You Said a Mouthful: *Tongue Twisters to Tangle, Titillate, Test and Tease* (Toluca Lake, CA: Dramaline Publications, 1991), 3.

5

Adapting Texts:
Drama/Narrative Fiction/Poetry

The "musical" metaphor has been mentioned by many group performance authorities when a text ultimately must be adapted into a
performance script.[1] Individual lines in a scripted text are like individual instruments in a band or orchestra. Sometimes a scripted line is
a brief solo melody, sometimes a duet or trio of "voices," and even
a full-fledged group "choral" or mass "voice." Chapters 5 and 6 will
provide options for "musicalizing" any literature, adapting texts into
a newly created art form.

General Adaptation Suggestions for All Literature

Though specific literary genres frequently call for unique textual adaptation, all texts can utilize generic conceptualizations for adaptation:
deletion, addition, repetition, rearrangement, extraction.

Usually the primary reason for *deletion* of lines or scenes is a time
constraint. However, every adaptor must cut or edit lines and scenes
while still remaining faithful to a production analysis and concept.
Deletion should begin with an overview of the entire text. Ask yourself the following questions to begin the process of deletion:

1. What is essential to know or feel in this text and cannot be cut?

2. What can be deleted without destroying the essential theme, tone, implied intent of the text?

3. Can the *tag lines* or "stage directions" be cut if performers actually do what is described? (Tag lines are the "he said/she said" descriptions in narrative fiction; stage directions are movement or emotional response requirements found in play formats.)

4. Can you eliminate minor characters or references to relatively unimportant subplots?

5. Can a narrative introduction summarize large amounts of text allowing you to "cut into" an episode rather than relying on "cutting out" material in an episode?

Deletion must never result in *deforming* a text. Keep what is essential to be faithful to a text's tone and essence. This deletion process can begin by xeroxing the actual text and doing pencil deletions initially. Take your pencil and strike through phrases you wish to eliminate. Use brackets in pencil to indicate sentences or phrases you plan to keep, followed by the passages you intend to delete. Do a second or third reading with colored highlighter pen(s) to determine essential elements to be retained. You may have to delete more at a later time, but those deletions should be minor adjustments at best. You will keep these pencil-marked copies until you determine that you can create an up-to-date, correct performance script.

Addition is not a license for rewriting an author's text, but should primarily be utilized after the deletion process. You add to a performance script a mere sentence or phrase to preserve continuity or acknowledge antecedent material necessary to know but deleted. If you delete a minor character, you can add a reference to him or her. Additions must be used to clarify, remove confusion, focus attention on the essential, and emphasize the important.

Repetition is a specialized form of addition and serves as an echo, a response, or a rhythmical reminder of what is important. Some texts are written with repetition originally included. Some scripted perform-ance texts may benefit from a repeating line, used for effect and impact.

Rearrangement is the reordering of the textual material. An adaptor may want to begin with the closing line, go back to the original arrange-ment, and repeat the introductory lines. Compiled or collage scripts may put together rearranged segments to contrast multiple texts. Make sure your production concept justifies your rearranging choices.

When a text is much too long to do in its entirety, you may use *extrac-tion* to focus only on one episode or scene. Extraction works best in an installment or scene that requires minimal explanatory comments or additions. Compiled or collage scripts rely heavily on extraction for creating a performance script.

Determining the division of textual lines into a performance script transforms any literary text into a dramatized format. As we will see later on, playwriting does this most obviously. But what other adaptive mechanisms for scripting can be used to create performable texts?

1. *Character Lines:* Each time a persona has dialogue have a per-former say it. You can have two or more performers offer a single character dialogue if your reason for doing so is to reveal layers of character, inward dialogue versus outward expressions, or even multiple personalities.

2. *Choral Lines:* More than one performer speaks simultaneously with another matching pitch, volume, tone, and rhythm so that a single or harmonic, perhaps even cacophonous, sound is suggested. An ancient dramatized practice, seen extensively in Greek drama, choral recitation has a vibrant use in group performance of literature. If you divided lines for one charac-ter between inner and outward expressions, choral reading could suggest that the inner and outward thoughts are one

83

and the same. This mechanism also work well as a culmination of solo to duet to trio to multiple line readings in narrative portions.

3. *Antiphonal Line*: A performer begins a phrase, and without pause, another performer completes the sentence or provides a side-by-side portion of a theme/idea that is then answered or finished by another performer. It is literally "one sound against another sound" to show interaction leading to completion.

4. *Interjection Line*: To emphasize a word, phrase, or idea, one performer can repeat a portion or offer a response between lines. The "call/response" interaction between a black preacher and the congregation is an example of this.

5. *Fade In/Fade Out Line*: Two performers can segue one to another in the middle of a line by gradually decreasing and increasing volume. Some portion may even be slightly choral, but the suggestion is a transfer of an idea to another. This line mechanism is especially effective if you want to imply that someone is sending a "letter" to another: One reads it as if writing it; the other picks up on it, reading it as if receiving it for the first time.

6. *Split Word Line*: This device is very difficult to accomplish without extensive rehearsal. Each performer states one word (even one syllable) of a line with tone and timing making it sound like one person reading one line. It is analogous to the rapid editing seen in music or film videos. Speech and tempo are at a normal speed and performers must learn timing and rhythms of speech to make it sound like one person speaking without halting or breaking.

7. *Cacophonous Line*: Two or more performers speak different words simultaneously in a sentence or phrase. Timing and practice is necessary to end simultaneously, even though what

is spoken is completely different. This technique has been used in modern musical theatre, such as the overlapping lyrical content of songs sung by the characters Jean Valjean and Inspector Javert in *Les Misérables*.

8. *Sound Effects Lines*: Either separated or overlayed, sound effects can be musical or auditory scripted responses/reactions to other lines.

With these generic line adaptation mechanisms in mind, we now move to a genre specific discussion of text to script maneuverings. We begin with drama because it is the easiest genre to adapt to performance opportunities.

Adapting Drama for Readers Theatre Scripts

One could assume that a play merely carries over its dialogue lines intact for a Readers Theatre script. But an adaptor may desire to further subdivide dialogue lines to incorporate many more performers. An adaptor could also interject choral responses or sound effects lines as well.

As mentioned in Chapter 3, contemporary plays may still require royalties and permission for any performance or even public reading. Classroom exercises are exempt from these restrictions by law, but if your production moves out and away from the classroom setting, you may face restrictions in how much (if at all) you may alter a dramatic text for presentation. Notations on the inside cover of acting booklets frequently state restrictions on performance as well as editing options. It may be necessary within a play to delete characters, lines of dialogue, and commentary from stage directions. If you do not choose to present an entire full-length, multi-act play in Readers Theatre format, you might consider other dramatic texts: the radio play, a revue skit, a one-act play, a short monologue or vignette, or an episode from a teleplay or screenplay.

Whatever line adaptations you incorporate, you should do the following:

1. Attempt to sustain and support the playwright's perspective and point of view.

2. Maintain focus on the basic characters embodied in the play script.

3. Offer a beginning, middle, and end to even a narrow portion from the larger work.

4. Create a narrator "voice" for expositional material deleted, but necessary for an audience to understand the script. You might sparingly add some expositional words to a character dialogue as an alternative.

5. Have performers state transitional words or phrases to clarify elements of the genre (e.g., "End of Act One," "Act Two/Scene One").

6. Avoid excessive uses of new material, even as transition devices. Let the text speak for itself in this transformed adaptation to Readers Theatre.

7. Keep from lulling an audience by breaking up long dialogue or monologue portions with other scripted response or repetitions. Rapid line delivery back and forth generates an interesting energy that is sensed by an audience.

Adapting Narrative Fiction into Chamber Theatre

Robert S. Breen, a professor at Northwestern University, claimed that narrative fiction (short stories and novels) shared so many qualities (e.g., story, characters, plot) in common with dramatic literature that it too could be adapted for public presentation without sacrificing any of the narrative elements. He likened his new theatrical technique to the intimate fashion of small ensemble orchestral works known as "chamber music." This *Chamber Theatre* became a specialized form of Readers Theatre and exclusively dramatized narrative fiction which "explores the relationship among characters in a narrative context provided by the narrator's intimate association with the audience."[2] First demonstrated on the campus of Northwestern in 1947, the Chamber Theatre approach to group performance of literature has progressed to the professional level with productions such as *Nicholas Nickleby* (1982), *The Grapes of Wrath* (1990), and *Travels With My Aunt* (1993). These professional examples also reveal that epic novels can be transformed into production spectacle and still retain the "Chamber Theatre" essence in individual episodes.

Breen's commitment to retaining the essential narrative portions led him to casting specific performers as narrators. These narrator personae would usually speak directly to audience members while other cast members primarily used onstage focus, as in conventional theatre. To retain the rhythm and pacing of the narration, Breen frequently left in the tag lines ("he said/she said") rather than delete them. But he admits that tag lines should be cut on some occasions once it is perfectly clear who is speaking or a sense of redundancy occurs.[3]

Early examples of Chamber Theatre adaptations seemed more closely connected to conventional theatre. Formal costuming and theatrical staging with actualized props and sets characterized these shows. With the evolution of Readers Theatre, the notions of Chamber Theatre seem less radical today. Chamber Theatre may have narrators use a symbolic notebook for the presence of a script, but all other character parts are memorized without script notebooks present.

Characteristics of Chamber Theatre

Only narrative fiction is dramatized.

Narrators are distinct performers.

Narrator(s) may or may not have a notebook script apparent.

Actualized costumes, props, sets, and lighting may be utilized.

Performers memorize lines.

Narrators deliver lines directly to the audience, but depending on the type of narration may look at performers using onstage focus.

Performers deliver lines to other performers using onstage focus.

Narrators may audibly say tag lines until clarity establishes the personae.

Figure 5.1

Text adaptation of narrative fiction must begin with an understanding of the type of narrator present. In what person does the narrator converse (i.e., first person, third person)? What is his or her degree of understanding and omniscience? In what tone or attitude does the narrator speak? Does the narrator always reveal the truth or is the narrative information sometimes unreliable due to bias? A first-person narrator's lines will need to be contrasted with actual dialogue if the narrator is also involved in the portrayal of a character in the story. An omniscient narrator can theoretically wander from audience to onstage focus while actual characters ignore the narrative presence. An objective narrator, who might also be offered in the third person, must maintain the allusion of merely reporting what occurs rather than trying to interpret the details. Sometimes lines could be divided so that an actual character speaks his/her own narrative assumptions.

Breen believed that a "stripped realism" and minimal set could, due to the richness of narrative fiction, make us of "the skillful management of words [to] conjure up images more satisfactorily than the stage or film studio with all its sophisticated resources."[4] He certainly was not opposed to highly theatrical productions of narrative fiction, but did not see theatricality as a prerequisite for the art form. Chamber Theatre productions seem to flourish in the found spaces of arena or thrust stages, rather than proscenium stages.

Chamber Theatre has a unique credo for script adaptation: "don't." "Don't cut anything unless, for the sake of the two hour traffic of the stage, you must abbreviate the original text."[5] However, narrative descriptions of actions performed by the actors can be eliminated. Other generic forms of script adaptation work creatively in dramatizing fiction as well.

If more than one performer represents a single character, then lines must be separated in a text to suggest various "selfs" or perspectives. Characters might also be combined or allowed to provide information that seems more narrative than character driven.

Narrative fiction adaptation may also change the linearity of the plotline. If you choose to adapt a text using "flashbacks," the plot sequences may of necessity require rearrangement. If you cut any scenes or characters, you may require the narrators to furnish the necessary information.

Breen concluded that Chamber Theatre was not interested in transforming short stories and novels into merely dialogue-driven exposition. He did not demand that any narrative fiction text be reformatted from the past tense into the present tense of most dramatic literature. He argued that by committing to the retention of the author's narrative voice, mechanisms such as setting, atmosphere, and motivations of characters could be highlighted and brought to life at the moment of action.[6] Therein lies the performable power and impact of Chamber Theatre.

Adapting Poetry/Song Lyrics to Performance

The nature of most poems (and even song lyrics) is that the rhythmic expression of human experience is usually brief, direct, with well-chosen, intensified language and imagery. The poetic form is in its essence difficult to edit, cut, or select apart from its totality. This is not an impossible barrier for the text adaptor. In fact, it may make adaptation easier.

An adaptor may not need to edit or cut stanzas of poetry. If the chosen poetic source is an epic poem (e.g., Stephen Vincent Benét's *John Brown's Body*), then an internal episode may be all the editing necessary for inclusion in a group performance of literature. However, if you must edit a stanza or series of words in a poem, work to maintain the rhythm and imagery of the poem's essence.

The general maxim for the performer of poetry is to present thought groups, not merely poetic lines. A script adaptor can write out these "thought groups" for individual or group performers so that the thought is clear, even if the poetic line has been altered in its original pattern.

As an adaptor you may want song lyrics to be audible without musical accompaniment, stressing the poetic text and imagery, or sung, maintaining the original connection to its musical origin. You may incorporate a technique used often in musical theatre productions called "talk sing," a chantlike rhythmic representation that does not actually resort to singing in its cadence.

Poetry in its entirety may not need a group voice. An adaptor may choose to include a poem or song lyric in a compiled text program as a monologue for a solo performance or even a transition to longer, more epic poems that call for multiple voicings.

If you must cut, delete, or edit conventional poetry (poetry with a pronounced rhythmic and rhyming pattern), cut in couplets or groupings of rhythm and rhyme. Rhythm in free verse is less predictable, but apparent nonetheless. Cut or delete free verse so that an established tone and rhythm is maintained.

Some poetry seems to be closer to prose. Dialogue lines create characters and thus, line divisions are more easily determined. As you work through the assignment in the Appendix dividing up lines in the prose poem, "The Changed Man" by Robert Phillips, consider how performers may or may not exclusively read narrative lines, but could also be linked to dialogue lines associated with an established persona(e).

Conclusion

All literature can implement a variety of generic editing or adaptation for performance devices. But complicated, "showy," technically difficult line divisions should not be used by an adaptor merely because he or she can. Ultimately, all literary adaptation must be tested for clarity and understanding. If a narrator voice speaks some lines because the tone or perspective has been identified, then the adaptor should consistently have the same narrator voice lines when that same tone or perspective is revisited. If a dramatic persona speaks in a dialogue to someone else, the group format demands that the responder be a different performer, not the original performer with altered voice. (An audience can expect that device in a solo performance format, but not in a group performance format.) If poetic lines are divided between performers, all performers must work in synchronicity to maintain rhythm and imagery notions.

Nonfiction literature and samples from an "oral" tradition are highly performable, but need scripting focus and direction also. In the following Chapter 6, the adaptor faces new challenges by creating mainly non-fiction scripts that although artificially scripted still have the sound and "presence" of that which is genuine and true-to-life.

Discussion and Assignments

1. Your instructor will divide you into groups of three or four students. You may be asked to work on these assignments overnight and bring them back to class or work on them in fifteen- to twenty-minute segments of your actual class time. Find the activity pages in the appendix that relate to narrative fiction, plays, and poetry. Take a pencil to the text and divide them into three or four performance parts, based on the number of people in your assignment group. (Readers 1 ,2, 3 or 4 can be designated in pencil by the number.) Share the different script adaptations and with minimal rehearsal, read them aloud within your group. Determine which adaptation variables best suit the genre of literature for clarity, consistency, and understanding. Why?

2. Why can an omniscient narrator use onstage focus as well as audience focus? Why should a third- person objective narrator avoid looking at performers onstage and merely maintain eye contact with audience members?

3. If you are not sure where your focus should be in a selection of poetry, what should be the default focal point? Why?

4. Why should you avoid long portions of solo performing in a Readers Theatre script, either in a monologue or in a narrative portion of a short story or novel?

5. What reasons could you see for rearranging the linearity [plot lines] of sequences for a performance of a short story or novel portion?

References

1. See: Marion L. Kleinau and Janet Larsen McHughes, *Theatres for Literature* (Sherman Oaks, CA: Alfred Publishing Company, 1980), 45–46; 54–55; Todd V. Lewis, *Communicating Literature: An Introduction to Oral Interpretation*—4th Edition (Dubuque, IA: Kendall/Hunt Publishing Company, 2004), 156; Judy E. Yordon, *Experimental Theatre: Creating and Staging Texts* (Prospect Heights, IL: Waveland Press, Inc., 1997), 32, 35.

2. Robert S. Breen, *Chamber Theatre* (Englewood Cliffs, NJ: Prentice Hall, Inc., 1978), 4.

3. Breen, *Chamber Theatre*, 4.

4. Breen, *Chamber Theatre*, 77.

5. Breen, *Chamber Theatre*, 86.

6. Breen, "Chamber Theatre," Supplement VII, *A Course Guide in the Theatre Arts at the Secondary School Level*, rev. ed. (Washington, D.C.: American Theatre Association, Inc., 1968), 107–108.

6

Adapting Texts: Nonfiction Prose/ Ethnographies/"Oral" Texts

Generic line division for adapting texts to performance holds true for other types of "literature" as well. In this chapter, we will explore unique challenges to these other types of texts as adaptors investigate options for group performance.

Adapting Nonfiction Prose for Readers Theatre

Prose literature that differs from a narrative structure includes such examples as: letters, essays, editorials, speeches, diaries, advertisements, and historical documents. The challenges for the adaptor begin with the need to find point of view and characterization (key narrative components) that may be elusive in these texts. These texts will engage an audience if there is an apparent potential for action or some evidence of conflict.

Letters can be arranged to tell a story or explain an ongoing relationship. Perhaps the two most famous dramatization of letters are Helene Hanff's *84, Charing Cross Road* (1970) and *Love Letters* (1990) by A. R. Gurney. The former is a play script of letters between Helene Hanff, Frank Doel, and other employees on the staff of the bookstore, Marks and Company in London. The latter play has two actors, male and female, exchanging letters of a romantic nature over several years. These particular scripts may need little to no alteration in their energetic and ingratiating approach to years of interaction and correspondence. Letters can also reveal awareness (e.g.. Martin Luther King, Jr.'s "Letter From the Birmingham Jail"). If a growing relationship between correspondents seems to be leading to aspects of intimacy, the "fade in/fade out" line division and delivery technique simulates the writing and receiving of such interchanges. In recent years prominent historical figures have had letters of correspondence published (e.g.. President Harry Truman's letters to his wife, Bess). Two readers could read and "receive" these letters in performance. Including this nonfiction type of literature can be a useful means to share a theme or topic in a compiled or collage performance script.

Essays may or may not have narrative components. Coger and White claimed that "to convert an essay into appropriate material for Readers Theatre, it is usually necessary to add characterization to the lines."[1] "Adding characterization" suggests that the adaptor should have a desired tone or approach that performers understand and endorse this approach. If the implied persona of an essay seems to be one person, the lines could still be divided among many to suggest the dimensionality of viewpoints espoused. What kind of characterizations would be necessary to embody the "voices" in this humorous essay by Dave Barry?

"Garbage Scan"
by Dave Barry

Monday morning. Bad traffic. Let's just turn on the radio here, see if we can get some good tunes, crank it up. Maybe they'll play some early Stones. Yeah. Maybe they...

—*Power On*—

"...just reached the end of 14 classic hits in a row, and we'll be right back after we..."

—Scan—

"...send Bill Doberman to Congress. Because Bill Doberman agrees with us. Bill Doberman. It's a name we can trust. Bill Doberman. It's a name we can remember. Let's write it down. Bill..."

—Scan—

"...just heard 19 uninterrupted classic hits, and now for this..."

—Scan—

"...EVIL that cometh down and DWELLETH amongst them, and it DID CAUSETH their eyeballs to ooze a new substance, and it WAS a greenish color, but they DID not fear, for they kneweth that the..."

—Scan—

"...followingisbasedonan800-yearleaseanddoesnotin-cludetaxtags-insuranceoranactualcarwegetyour-house-andyourchildrenandyourkidneys..."

—Scan—

"NINE THOUSAND DOLLARS!!! BUD LOOTER CHEVROLET OPEL ISUZU FORD RENAULT JEEP CHRYSLER TOYOTA STUDEBAKER TUCKER HONDA WANTS TO GIVE YOU, FOR NO GOOD REASON..."

—Scan—

"...Bill Doberman. He'll work for you. He'll *fight* for you. If people are rude to you, Bill Doberman will *kill* them. Bill Doberman..."

—Scan—

"…enjoyed those 54 classic hits in a row, and now let's pause while…"

—*Scan*—

"…insects DID swarm upon them and DID eateth their children, but they WERE NOT afraid, for they trustedeth in the…"

—*Scan*—

"…listening audience. Hello?"

"Hello?"

"Go ahead."

"Steve?"

"This is Steve. Go ahead."

"Am I on?"

"Yes. Go ahead."

"Is this Steve?"

—*Scan*—

"This is Bill Doberman, and I say convicted rapists have *no business* serving on the Supreme Court. That's why, as your congressman, I'll make sure that…"

—*Scan*—

"…GIVE YOU SEVENTEEN THOUSAND DOLLARS IN TRADE FOR ANYTHING!!! IT DOESN'T EVEN HAVE TO BE A CAR!!! BRING US A ROAD KILL!!! WE DON'T CARE!!! BRING US A CANTALOUPE-SIZED GOB OF EAR WAX!!! BRING US…"

—*Scan*—

"...huge creatures that WERE like winged snakes EXCEPT they had great big suckers, which DID cometh and pulleth their limbs FROM their sockets liketh this, 'Pop,' but they WERE not afraid, nay they WERE joyous, for they had..."

—*Scan*—

"...just heard 317 uninterrupted classic hits, and now..."

—*Scan*—

"Bill Doberman will shrink your swollen membranes. Bill Doberman has..."

—*Scan*—

"...glowing bodies strewn all over the road, and motorists are going to need..."

—*Scan*—

"...FORTY THOUSAND DOLLARS!!! WE'LL JUST GIVE IT TO YOU!!! FOR NO REASON!!! WE HAVE A BRAIN DISORDER!!! LATE AT NIGHT, SOMETIMES WE SEE THESE GIANT GRUBS... AND WE HEAR THESE VOICES SAYING..."

—*Scan*—

"Steve?"

"Yes."

"Steve?"

"Yes."

"Steve?"

—*Scan*—

"Yes, and their eyeballs DID explode like party favors, but they WERE NOT sorrowful, for they kneweth…"

—Scan—

"Bill Doberman. Him good. Him heap strong. Him your father. Him…"

—Scan—

"…finished playing 3,814 consecutive classic hits with no commercial interruptions dating back to 1978, and now…"

—Scan—

"…the radiation cloud is spreading rapidly, and we have unconfirmed reports that…"

—Scan—

"…getting sleepy. Very sleepy. When you hear the words 'Bill Doberman,' you will…"

—Power Off—

OK, never mind. I'll just drive. Listen to people honk. Maybe hum a little bit. Maybe even, if nobody's looking, do a little singing. [Singing quietly]

*I can't get nooooooo
Sa-tis-FAC-shun…*

I included this essay in my oral interpretation textbook as a solo performance piece,[2] but I think it works better and is even funnier as a group performance piece. Do you agree? Look for other essayists' works and transform these nondramatic short pieces into compelling moments for audiences.

Editorials mainly appear in newspapers and magazines and are pointedly rhetorical. Authors of editorials have a viewpoint and desire to persuade readers to support their perspectives. Some editorials make insightful well-reasoned arguments; others seem like meandering rantings. One can find editorials in the "opinion" section of newspapers or magazines. One can also receive transcripts of televised editorial commentaries made by national pundits such as Andy Rooney (*60 Minutes*) or Rush Limbaugh or a local newscaster in a locality. How might you divide up the lines and dramatize this editorial by Dennis Palumbo?

"You Want Mind-Blowing? Look at the Middle-Aged Brain"
by Dennis Palumbo

On the pages of medical journals and the cover of *Time* magazine, in feature stories on network news and nightly jokes in Jay Leno's monologue, there's been a swell of media coverage this past year concerning "the teenage brain."

Despite sounding like the title of Hollywood's latest horror-movie blockbuster, the phrase actually refers to recent neurological research on adolescent brain chemistry. It's finally been demonstrated empirically (to the surprise of practically no one not wearing a lab coat) that the teenage brain is different from that of a mature adult.

According to the data, these differences explain the average teen's inclination to stay up late, sleep until noon and exhibit extreme mood swings (for example, from sullen and defiant to *really* sullen and defiant). Some researchers have even blamed these brain differences for the adolescent's inexplicable devotion to high-decibel music, low-decibel mumbling and the piercing of unlikely body parts.

As soon as these results made national headlines, the usual social pundits—bored with Iraq, the Supreme

Court nominee and Jessica Simpson's divorce—began hitting the TV talk-show circuit. This new research, they claimed, clearly suggested that we should ban teen driving and even raise the voting age. After all, we now had proof positive that today's teens are simply too erratic to be entrusted with such responsibilities.

This may be. But what about the *midlife* brain? Perhaps the next time we embark on exhaustive, heavily funded research into what's in the human skull, we should focus our efforts on the average middle-aged person— because if my friends and I are at all representative, I'd argue that whatever's going on in our collective brains is equally suspect.

Though not without good reason. Most adults I know are overworked, over-stressed and generally overwhelmed from their daily struggles with careers, child-rearing and relationships. They're forgetful, continually on a diet, obsessed with their health (popping pills to an extent no teenager would even contemplate), envious of their neighbors and co-workers, and always—always—sleep-deprived. Frankly, even on a good day our brains are nothing to write home about. It's everything we can do to keep our complicated, must-have Starbucks coffee orders straight in our heads.

I think it's too easy to blame all this on brain chemistry. The truth is, life is hard, no matter how old you are. Whether you're worried about making the track team or paying the mortgage, about fitting in with the cool kids or impressing your new boss, it's about trying to cope.

Granted, your average teen's coping mechanisms may rarely extend beyond junk food and video games. But are adults' choices any better? Addicted to Internet porn, "Desperate Housewives," Tom Clancy novels and golf. Running from their yoga class to a Parents Without Partners meeting to the latest Donald Trump get-rich-quick seminar. And, between all this, compulsively checking e-mails and sending text messages on their cell phones (all the while nursing fantasies of winning the lottery, or running off to Tahiti with the office manager).

Let's face it, teens have just two basic goals: having sex and getting into a good college. Both are pretty laudable and straight-forward aims, especially when compared with the confusing and relentless demands of contemporary life with which grownups have to contend. It's no wonder that at the end of the day, most adults just want to collapse on the sofa and channel-surf.

Sartre once said that the state of modern man is incomprehension and rage. OK, maybe he was a bit of a Gloomy Gus. But isn't the bewilderment and struggle to which he alludes true at times for all of us, particularly at certain crucial stages in our life?

As a psychotherapist, I see daily the unfortunate consequences of assigning a diagnostic label to practically every kind of behavior under the sun. We need to remember that people are too complex to fit neatly into categories. Otherwise, we risk turning every character trait, coping mechanism and idiosyncrasy into a pathology. Let's not use these latest clinical data on adolescent brain chemistry, no matter how compelling, to do the same to teens—to reduce to a syndrome the myriad ways they struggle to cope with a very difficult developmental stage in a complex and often contradictory world.

And before we start debating whether teens should be allowed to drive and vote, we'd better be able to defend letting us adults do so. It's not as if our record in either of these endeavors is anything to brag about.

In other words, give the kids a break. They're not responsible for the way their brains develop, any more than they are for the world in which they have to grow up. The latter is the result of brains much older, and supposedly wiser, than theirs.

You might have the same performer say lines that begin with the first-person pronoun "I," but divide up the other portions for the performing ensemble. Would you use any choral reading? Which other adaptation mechanisms might work effectively as well?

Speeches need not be solo monologues delivered by one performer because one person originally delivered the speech. Consider the line division of this famous address by President Abraham Lincoln, adapted to ensemble presentation from the original one persona speech:

The Gettysburg Address
(November 19, 1863)
by President Abraham Lincoln

(Four Performers: 1, 2, 3, 4; two or more numbers
    together read simultaneously)

2:    "Fourscore and seven years ago our fathers
        brought forth on this continent

12:    a new nation—

1:    Conceived in liberty,

3:    and dedicated to the proposition that

ALL: all men are created equal.

4:    Now we are engaged in a great civil war,

1:    testing whether that nation,

3:    or any nation so conceived and so dedicated,

13:    can long endure.

4:    We are met on a great battlefield of that war.

2:     We have come to dedicate a portion of that field as a final resting place

3:     for those who here gave their lives that that nation might live.

ALL: It is altogether fitting and proper that we should do this.

1:     But, in a larger sense, we cannot dedicate,

4:     we cannot consecrate,

2:     we cannot hallow this ground.

3:     The brave men,

23:    living and dead,

2:     who struggled here,

1:     have consecrated it far above our poor power to add or detract.

3:     The world will little note nor long remember what we say here,

124:   but it can never forget what they did here.

4:     It is for us, the living, rather, to be dedicated here

1:     to the unfinished work which they who fought here

4:     have thus far so nobly advanced.

3:     It is rather for us to be here dedicated to the great task remaining before us,

2:     that from these honored dead we take increased devotion to that cause

3:	for which they gave the last full measure of devotion;
234:	that we here highly resolve
1:	that these dead shall not have died in vain;
234:	that this nation, under God,
1:	shall have a new birth of freedom,
2:	and that government
3:	of the people,
24:	by the people,
234:	for the people,
ALL:	shall not perish from the earth.

How do line divisions bring to life onstage a nonfiction literary example such as a speech? What dynamically happens to a text, originally offered in solo voice but now adapted for ensemble voices?

Diaries must contain a story line, reveal character motivations and perspectives, and unveil new perceptions. Mark Twain's engaging essay, written in diary form, reveals thoughts on the human condition and the relationships of the sexes in *Adam's Diary* and *Eve's Diary*. *The Diary of Anne Frank* was a diary first before it was turned into a play and film screenplay.

Advertisements can transition to public performance as originally offered or be redivided for ensemble. Print advertisements will rely on language while televised advertisements will have the dramatic quality already apparent. Familiarity can also make the performance of advertisements fun and even thought-provoking for an audience. If thematic elements in prominent advertisements coincide with the program theme in your production guide, then the advertisement elements could make for interesting transition material.

Historical documents are politically written or transcribed artifacts that are rich in varieties of language and frequently reasoned argument. Reading from the Sharia, the Islamic law that calls for strict punishment by death for any Muslim who converts to another religion, may serve as a controversial portion of a group performance on issues of tolerance. Some "captured" debate interactions from *The Congressional Record* may focus attention on the arguments pro and con for a political or social issue. Manifestos for a variety of causes articulate arguments for performance as well.

Nonfiction literature can have inherent dramatic qualities, but the adaptor must discover them and assemble them in a manner that calls forth the performable aspects. Some adaptors have also found nonfiction elements to serve as insightful transition materials to connect other dramatized texts.

Adapting Ethnographies and Oral Texts for Readers Theatre

While most other literary texts evolve into presentational art forms, the presentation of "real-life" excerpts attempts to re-create faithful "representations" of such diverse "oral" samples as results in transcript form of field studies, everyday conversation elements, and documentaries with interviews as well as stand-up comedy routines. Personal narratives of your own life story also can be dramatized by this representational format. Readers Theatre could offer such diverse "oral" texts as transcripts of an Alcoholics Anonymous meeting, a fan conversation at a Star Trek convention, a personal narrative of your first visit to the Department of Motor Vehicles at the age of sixteen, or the monologue of a comedian on Comedy Central.

These nontraditional texts are gaining in popularity as performance options for groups and can work as a complete single scripted text or as part of a compiled or collage script. Performance studies practitioners are leading the way in studying the performance aspects of these nontraditional texts. Anthropology studies seem to be driving this interest in describing everyday existence and what that existence sounds like. Ethnography is a field study of various cultures with samples of cultural interaction and performance worthy of duplication in a public sphere as well as analytical study. We have previously suggested that the analysis of a text precedes performance. When you move into the realm of performing ethnographies, you begin with observation of a culture, recording samples of that culture, and performing the original performance as accurately and completely as possible.[3] Ethical considerations are paramount as you not only gain permission to "represent" the culture, but attempt to do the impossible: represent comprehensively the culture and its communicative nuances fairly, respectfully, and without bias or prejudice. This is the ultimate challenge for the adaptor/director of ethnographic performance materials.

Robert Hopper of the University of Texas at Austin has embraced a symbolic system that attempts to re-create the original performance of everyday conversation. While these conversation scripts look much like a play script, the attempt to reproduce exactly the original presentation changes the dynamics of actor involvement. The task for the adaptor/director of conversation as performance is to transcribe a recorded message and transform it into a scriptlike form. Hopper also suggests that in rehearsal the actors speak in unison with the original recording to match the performance accuracy as closely as possible, as well as enhance memorization.[4] These kinds of conversational performances tend to have more overlapping lines, even running your lines into the previous actor's lines.

A fascinating transcribed example of conversational performance may be found in Richard Buttny and Arthur D. Jensen's essay, "Hot-Stove Talk," that reveals the fan talk of men who love baseball, particularly the statistics and relationships necessary to compete in a duel of one-upsmanship in a communication encounter:

> D: So you guys you guys like the Padres don't you in the N.L. West right?
>
> C: Or the Dodgers
>
> D: I like the Dodgers
>
> A: the Dodgers
>
> D: I think the Padres are a good team? I like you know talk about a deal you know that works both ways for each team, ah Sanders for Hitchcock trade they got Hitchcock now? but I still think the Dodgers ya know talk about good farm systems it seems like they're always coming up with a new study every
>
> B: The rookie of the year three years in a row

D: Ah definitely and I mean hey you know Martinez Nomo ya know even Candiotti? I mean Park Chan Ho Park

B: Well yeah I think if anything's going to win the division

C: Valdes

D: Ishmael Valdes Greg Lahoya

A: The only thing that bothers me about the Dodgers they have a great pitching staff right? but year after year it always it always comes down to them trying to hit the ball out of the park, they never seem to have a lineup that's ah has multi-purposes like look at the Braves, ya look at them they have guys that— McGriff can hit the ball out of the park but he also can drive in with a single they've guys—it seems like Karros I picture—I think he's an all or nothing hitter, year after year he hits twenty-eight home runs but he bats two fifty

C: Write this down I think the biggest off-season mistake the Dodgers made was signing Karros to a long-term contract Piazza's knees are going to go and they're gonna have to have to move Piazza sooner or later

A: Plus he's so bad defensively he doesn't

D: I mean they'll they'll be alright DHing him every once and a while ya know but they really—they should have tried and go out

B: Yeah

D: and get like a Chris Widger from a—from Seattle who was traded to Montreal in the Sierra deal to a young catching defensive prospect?

> B: Right
>
> D: And honestly dealt Karros for a leadoff hitter or
>   something ya know I mean like you said I think
>   Karros is over-rated ya know.
>
> B: They need another bat
>
> From *Take Me Out to the Ballgame: Communicating Baseball* , edited by Gumpert and
> Drucker. Copyright © 2002 by Hampton Press, Inc. Reprinted by permission.

A transcription may require symbols with definitions to match the overlapping or inflections of conversations and symbols were not included above to reveal the challenge in representing conversations. Grammar does not have to make sense. Repetition seems to be rampant. Thoughts are rarely complete. Yet, the conversation with code words and "culture speak" seems to ultimately make sense when performed.

Our culture that embraces the norm of cable television networks and multichannel optional programming also sees recording as normative. VHS tape recorders are passé, yet still being produced. DVD recorders or TiVo are the expected additions to any household cable or satellite connection. The ability to record "oral" texts from documentary interviews to stand-up comedy routines leads to opportunities to transfer these recordings into a performance script. It may be tedious to play a portion, repeat it as you type it into your computer, but sophisticated software can hear even a recorded message or transcript and type in the transcript. The technology that brings SAP or simultaneous print-outs for the deaf to the television screen could easily adapt "oral" texts into performance scripts. Personal life stories recorded as part of documentaries no longer need languish in anonymity once a documentary has aired or made its way through the art cinema house circuit. Of course, a documentary like *March of the Penguins* might be a bit dull for a theatrical audience, but you never know what creative adaptors/ directors can do with the rich options of nonfiction and oral texts.

<u>Conclusion</u>

While fiction, drama, and poetic literature purport to present reality, the nonfiction and oral traditions actually "represent" reality. These rich texts preserve various cultural heritages. They give people opportunities to tell their own stories to others who hopefully find connection and similarities with their own experiences. Technology has truly made us once more a global village, replete with opportunities to hear and tell our own stories as we discover that as human beings we share much more in common and we have far fewer differences than we might think.

Discussion and Assignments

1. Your instructor will divide you into groups of three or four students. You may be asked to work on these assignments overnight and bring them back to class or work on them in fifteen- to twenty-minute segments of your actual class time. Individually take the Dave Barry essay or the newspaper editorial text on "teenage brains" and divide it into performance lines for three or four actors. (Readers 1, 2, 3, or 4 can be designated in pencil by the number.) Share the different script adaptations and with minimal rehearsal, read them aloud within your group. What dynamics were at work to make these nonfiction texts dramatic, humorous, and interesting to perform? Why?

2. Assign the "Gettysburg Address" speech to each member in a group of four (or reassign the numbers if you have other numbers of actors within your small group). How does the group performance of a speech delivered by a single person change the perception of the original text? Does it make it more or less dramatic and interesting? Does the group need to be exclusively male to make the Abraham Lincoln speech make sense?

3. Assign at least one group of three women from your class to present to the class the ethnographic excerpt, found in the Appendix, of Kate Millet's *The Prostitution Papers: A Candid Dialogue* (New York: Avon Books, 1973). Divide up the lines so that you have the text presented as a monologue, a duologue, and as a trio performance. What makes this nonfiction text seem more real than a fictionalized account of prostitution?

4. Would women, interested in sports, have a different type of conversational dynamic than the four men who converse about baseball? What would be different if the genders were mixed?

5. Write a five-minute scripted version of a personal narrative, based on an episode from your own experience. Divide the lines so that three people could present the personal narrative. Practice the presentation in class sessions and choose several for class presentations.

6. Divide up the baseball conversation text for four men, practice it, and present it to your group or class. How do you know where to place emphasis or even pause or use grammatical sense when the transcript does not always match up to formal rules of written English grammar or essay writing? Would you interrupt or overlap lines in any place? Why?

7. Name at least four cultures and a communication encounter that would make for an interesting dramatized performance. Name at least four examples of documentaries that could be highly dramatic. Name two or three stand-up comedians and their routines that would translate well to a performance venue with a group performing the lines.

Additional Reading

Langelier, Kristin. "From Text to Social Context." *Literature in Performance* 6,1 (April 1986): 67.

Langelier, Kristin M. "Personal Narratives: Perspectives on Theory and Research." *Text and Performance Quarterly* 9,4 (1989): 243–276.

Randall, Deleasa M. "Staged Replication of Naturally Occurring Talk: A Performer's Perspective." *Text and Performance Quarterly* 13,2 (April 1993): 194.

Saville-Troike, Muriel. *The Ethnography of Communication: An Introduction* 2nd Edition. (Oxford: Blackwell, 1989).

Turner, Victor. *The Anthropology of Performance.* New York: PAJ Publications, 1986.

References

1. Leslie Irene Coger and Melvin R. White, *Readers Theatre Handbook: A Dramatic Approach to Literature*—3rd Edition. (Glenview, IL: Scott, Foresman and Company, 1982), 52.

2. Todd V. Lewis, *Communicating Literature: An Introduction to Oral Interpretation*, 4th Edition. (Dubuque, IA: Kendall/Hunt Publishing Company, 2004), 104–106.

3. Judy E. Yordon, *Experimental Theatre: Creating and Staging Texts* (Prospect Heights, IL: Waveland Press, Inc., 1997), 191–193.

4. Robert Hopper, "Dramatic Performance of Everyday Conversation," in Paul H. Gray and James VanOosting, *Performance in Life and Literature* (Boston: Allyn and Bacon, 1996), 237–241.

7

Designing and Staging
the Textual Performance

While the elements of design and staging for a Readers Theatre production can hopefully captivate an audience, "a very beautiful, highly imaginative setting will have no particular value in a Readers Theatre production if it has little or no relation to the text being performed."[1] Set pieces, costuming, precision movements, and fascinating creativity in blocking cannot be a part of the production merely to dazzle or because you can "pull off" the flashy spectacle. You should not move just to be able to move. Every design and staging element must always justify itself by its ability to feature the performance of text.

Since the adaptor/director has already engaged an analysis of the texts to be performed, a *production concept* should emerge that will help guide the choices for design and staging. This "vision" of what the production could become begins the design and staging process.

Casting

The production concept will provide an initial focus to the number and gender of performers cast to present a text or texts. Readers Theatre-type presentations, however, do not require nor should you assume traditional forms of casting. Male and female character parts or non-gender-specific narrative portions can be cast by availability, skill, or adaptor/director decision rather than by demographics such as age or gender.

Although by definition Readers Theatre productions involve two or more cast members, realities of design and blocking, not to mention rehearsal logistics, are always factors to be reckoned. Blocking and staging variables tend to be minimized when a cast has two to four members. Casts of eight or more may accentuate creative options, but matching schedules for rehearsals becomes more difficult and seems to increase exponentially as the cast size increases. Large casts also make movement difficult if the found space is small or restricted in some manner. Creative variations in design and blocking seem most manageable and effective when a cast totals four to six members for a Readers Theatre production.

An adaptor/director should anticipate the performance space options and create a cast number based on the logistics. If you have a "traveling" Readers Theatre production, then adjustments to blocking and movement will be determined by the available space. If the usual found space is restricted, then the only way a larger cast can be accommodated is to constrict the actual playing area and block vertically rather than horizontally. I will explain more about how to do this in the section on *Movement* in this chapter.

Casts of four to six members make design and blocking most manageable.

Performance Space

The most widely used performance space is the *proscenium*. The
playing area may or may not have a curtain, but the rectangular box
playing area with "wings" has a clear separation from the audience
seated in front of them, usually in raked seating configurations that
deter obstructed views (See Figure 7.1.)

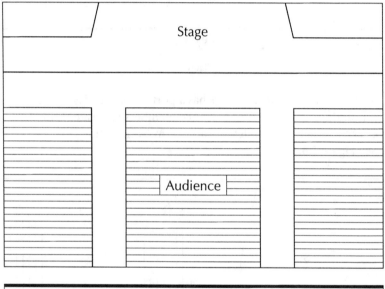

Proscenium Stage

Figure 7.1

A variation of the proscenium configuration is the *alley stage*. In this
space, the rectangular box playing area is in the center with audience
members seated above and below (relative to the centrist playing area)
but not stage left or stage right of the performers. This two-side configuration requires that performers turn their back to half of the audience
at certain times (See Figure 7.2.)

Audience
Stage
Audience

Alley Stage

Figure 7.2

The *thrust* or *three-quarter stage* has a portion of the playing area behind the performers, but audience members are seated and observe the action from left, right, and in front of the performers (See Figure 7.3.)

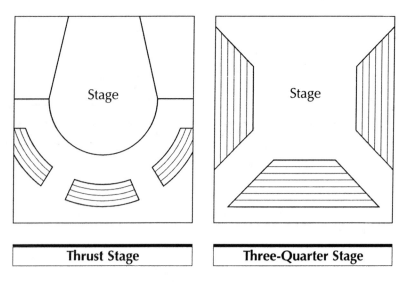

Thrust Stage	**Three-Quarter Stage**

Figure 7.3

The *arena stage* (also called *theatre-in-the-round*) has the playing area centralized with the audience seated on all sides. Performers must vary blocking so that each side of the audience sees performers at some time (See Figure 7.4.)

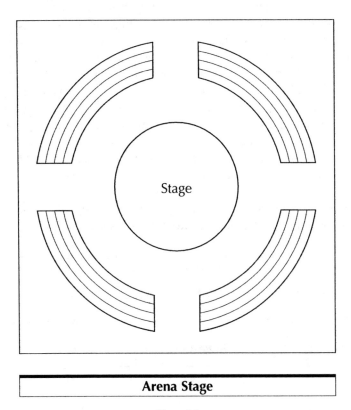

Arena Stage

Figure 7.4

Newer, more experimental uses of space may ask an audience to always be mobile, moving to different locations of a performance space as the performers mingle and interact (e.g., staged murder mysteries or "weddings as theatre" with scripted and improvisational dialogue at a "house" transformed into a found space theatre).

Some performance spaces emphasize certain kinds and types of focus over others. The proscenium and alley stages obviously foster more representational focal points (i.e., onstage focus). The thrust, three-quarter, and arena staging spaces accentuate the intimacy of the audience in proximity and thus foster audience focus when appropriate. These spaces do not exclude onstage or offstage focus, but with closeness to the audience the challenge to locate offstage interaction points becomes noteworthy. The performer must find an offstage location between audience members rather than above their heads. Movement and body angles seem to be more widely used when the playing space is surrounded by audience members since at any given moment a performer will have his/her back to someone in the audience. The focus points for performances with a mobile audience are shared between onstage and audience focus as actors amalgamate audience and cast members into an integrated whole for the theatrical engagement.

For the traditional proscenium and thrust/three-quarter playing spaces, the performance area is divided into nine quadrants (See Figure 7.5.)

Performance Areas		
Upstage R	Upstage Center	Upstage L
Center Stage R	Center Stage	Center Stage L
Downstage R	Downstage Center	Downstage L

Figure 7.5

For other performance areas (alley, arena, mobile), the grid is constantly shifting. The most powerful and compelling performance quadrant is *center stage*. It represents the "strongest" performance area because our attention is automatically drawn to center areas. Directors should place important characters and scenes at center stage. Scenes placed left or right of the center stage need to be used also so as to maintain audience interest, provide variety for audience viewing perspectives, and prevent lulling predictability to staging locations. Downstage areas are usually strong and are the areas closest to the audience. Right and left designations are always made from the performer's viewpoint. Upstage positioning is generally perceived as weaker, not receiving an abundance of attention. Upstage locations serve well for supportive personae, background narrators, observers, or as a retreat for those who are momentarily out of a scene.

Movement on Stage

When should performers move? Perhaps a better question is *"Why should performers move?"* The answer to both questions centers on textual clues and textual transitions. All stage movements and relocation of personnel and properties should seem motivated and the text itself will usually generate a meaningful decision. For example, if a text says, "The next morning,…" it would make sense to relocate on the line since the text indicates a change in day and possibly a location.

One performer should not move in front of another performer, especially if the performer speaking has audience focus. This disrupts the focal plane. As a rule, however, people should move to new locations or formations while someone, usually presenting a narrative portion, is delivering the line; what a performer does is move behind the performer. "Dead air" silence as you move halts the flow and continuity of any performance. Performers can even move stage properties while performing to new formations to sustain the flow of the production also. A performer could say lines while moving properties or do so while another performer has lines to speak.

All theatrical staging movement embraces the notion that visual perception seeks variety, counterbalancing positions, as well as grouped clusters. The most boring and uninteresting formation on any stage is the straight line facing the audience, although every production will probably have brief moments of straight line usage (and this does not include any "curtain calls" after the production is complete). It does need to be said that "lines" in and of themselves are not dull when altered by angles or circles or various geometric shapes. The concept of *obliquity* creates a perceived tension that is healthy in all blocking decisions. An oblique line is neither perpendicular nor parallel; it may even be slanting. Obliquity creates the perception that the greater the angle of deviating lines, the greater is the movement perceived.[2]

To best understand stage movement variables consider three axis planes or dimensions: *x*, *y*, and *z*. The "x" axis consists of the stage right to center to left positions. Performers A, B, C, and D can be placed along an imaginary line as shown in Figure 7.6.

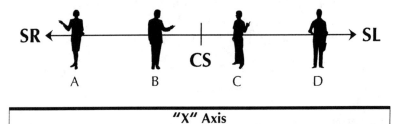

"X" Axis

Figure 7.6

(It is the dreaded "straight" line, but the "x" axis will be invigorated by subsequent discussion and application.)

The "x" axis appears rigid and non-dynamic in perception of energy.

124

The "y" axis dimension moves the performers upstage to downstage, along the continuum shown in Figure 7.7.

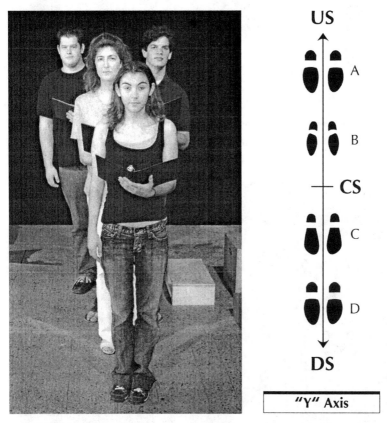

US

A

B

CS

C

D

DS

"Y" Axis

The "y" axis creates a dynamic quality of stage depth in its cast picture.

Figure 7.7

The "z" axis plane uses vertical space. By using height variation of blocks, sets, stools, platforms, and ladders, performers move along the path shown in Figure 7.8.

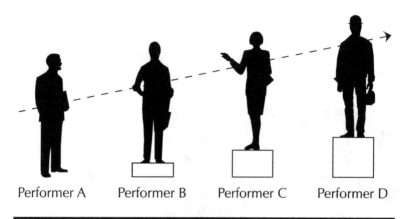

Performer A   Performer B   Performer C   Performer D

"Z" Axis

Figure 7.8

Height differences using boxes and platforms create staging variety on the "z" axis.

If the found space is restricted, the director can block actions and groupings along the "z" axis to make the most of limited performance areas to the left and to the right.

Effective blocking seeks to establish *stage pictures* comprised of combinations and variations of these dimensional axis planes. Angles of bodies, cluster groupings, curving formations, and various geometric shapes (e.g., squares, triangles, circles, oblongs) create visually appealing stage configurations.

To counteract the lack of perceived dynamism in straight lines along the "x" axis that faces the audience, bend the angle of the straight line in combination with "y" or "z" axis planes. Obliquity assists audience perceptions because of the combinations and variations of these interacting dimensional planes. As you intersect these performance planes, you will need to keep taller performers in back of shorter performers or compensate with height adjustments from set pieces.

No one should be blocked out of view if an ensemble cluster stage picture is created.

That being said, at times some performers in a cluster group may be obscured from the sight line of a particular audience member's seat location. This may be unavoidable for a short duration. Generally, a director should stage a scene for those who will perceive from a centered seating perspective. Movement to other locations and stage area formations in natural transition places can assure that most audience members can see most performers a majority of the overall production time period.

This need to move seems exacerbated when the area is arena, thrust, three-quarter, or mobile formatted. But movement for the sake of movement seems too busy and is definitely distracting. You do not want people in the audience to become enamored with the movement and not pay attention to the language of the text. Movement decisions are ideal if the audience is unaware of the magnitude of the changes.

Combinations of axis planes and clusters enhance stage pictures in scene blocking.

Smooth and subtle movement furthers the aesthetic beauty in this artistic format.

One particular movement technique that seems to work when sparingly used in Readers Theatre productions is a *group "military precision" movement*. These movements are the theatrical equivalent of boot camp or rifle drills or simultaneous kinesic behaviors. Some examples include: cast members with scripts turning pages at precisely the same time; narrators turning in and out of scenes at exactly the same time and angle; people sitting or crossing their legs or standing at the same time. This technique can be effective, but as Liesel Reinhart of Mount San Antonio College reminds us:

> I don't think there's a necessity any more for theatres where every head tilt, every step, every breath are synchronized. I think that was a trend in the 90s for a while and I think it is largely over. The only time that approach really makes sense to audiences is if the material calls for that kind of synchronicity—maybe a military theme, for instance—or there is an overall aesthetic effect gained from the style that complements the text (a theatre about mathematics, for instance). It would be odd to see a Readers Theatre about a disease or social issue where the performers are overly coordinated and robotic while the characters they are portraying are confused and very human.[3]

Most Readers Theatre productions are designed with staging that keeps most performers in close proximity stage pictures. If the text has quick, short lines between performers or groups and the staging has these performers at far extremes of stage left and right, the audience may have to move their heads as if at a "tennis match" and too much of this eventually "hurts" the audience's necks. Even if your found space is more rectangular (SL to SR) than deep (US to DS), keep the angles, formations, and clusters more centralized to the playing area available to you.

If a director needs to simulate the passage of time or the sensation that time has stopped, certain movements help relay information about time:

1. **Freeze:** Remaining motionless tells an audience that time has momentarily stopped. When you resume action or break the freeze, time begins again.

2. **Slow Motion:** It can comedically or dramatically appear to portray rapid movement slowed down to highlight physical activity.

3. **In-Place Movement:** It gives the impression of walking or running without leaving the spot. Such motions are suggested and understood as connected to time passage by the audience.

4. **Accelerated Movement:** Fast movements, similar to an old silent movie, speed up time in a surreal manner.

Some staging concepts for a Readers Theatre production do not call for performers to ever exit the playing area. However, certain entrance or exit techniques suggest your presence or absence from a scene:

1. **Bowed Heads:** Dropping your chin so that it hits your chest communicates that you are out of the scene. Raising your head brings you back into the scene;

2. **Turn In, Out, or Around:** Turning your back to an audience removes you from view and the scene. Turning to full or half front stances serves as an entrance or possibly a scene change. Multiple narrators that enter a scene should turn left to right (or vice versa) in choreographed precision if so desired.

3. **Moving to a New Scene Location:** By walking to a new portion of the found space, you signal that you are performing a different persona, or that a new location now exists for the next episode.

4. *Stand or Sit*: When you do either of these actions, coupled with others indicated above, you signal an entrance or an exit;

5. *Lighting*: A spotlight or flashlight or candlelight can bring you in or out of a scene.

Stage Properties

Since Readers Theatre seeks to activate audience imaginations, an adaptor/director may not always opt for actualized set pieces. Symbolic set pieces may better serve a production because of creative multiuse. Stools, blocks, chairs, crates, benches, platforms, and ladders may help cluster groupings, height variables on the "z" axis, and other stage areas.

Boxes or platforms using plywood and painted black or colors associated with the productions need to be of varying size and height. Construction of 18 by 18 by 10 inch, 18 by 18 by 14 inch, and 18 by 18 by 18 inch units are not only easy to build and paint, but they are light and can be moved by performers during the actual show.

Boxes and stools of varying heights can assist in creative blocking options.

If a set piece must sustain two or more adults, it should remain stationary; smaller boxes or platforms, built to support one adult's weight, are more portable. Stairs can be constructed for group clusters, or several height variable boxes can be moved together to form stairs. Ladders or unfinished stools can be purchased from local home construction stores. Help the audience to imagine by utilizing creativity in the integration of multi-function set pieces.

Scripts Present or Absent

Determine if three-ring binder notebooks will be present and symbolically referenced or used as props. If scripts are absent, still discover ways to make the Readers Theatre presentational during certain aspects of a performance.

Sometimes the production concept may call for a scriptlike prop to be present, but not in the form of a binder notebook. Scripted "newspapers" or "architectural blueprints" are two examples of "scripts" that could be occasionally visible or stuffed away in shirts or back pockets.

If notebook scripts are to be used, the 7 by 9 inch three-ring binder notebook is the easiest to hold and use in a production. Such a notebook could be cradled at times in one hand. To cut down on the crinkling sound of page turning, cast members may wish to invest in clear vinyl page holders. By inserting your scripted text back to back you can reduce the page turns to a minimum as well.

If scripts in notebooks are to be present and referenced, consider using these scripts as props. A notebook could be cradled as a baby, used as car steering wheel, opened and used by multiple performers as walls or barriers, or any other creatively imagined tool, device, or set piece.

Costuming

Chamber Theatre productions frequently have actualized costuming with narrators distinctly set apart by unique dress and appearance (unless the narrators are also characters in the adapted text). The default colors for most Readers Theatre productions for a class presentation (not usually a forensics competition) are black and white, but this is certainly not a requirement.

Some production concepts might ask performers to add small costuming additions to establish new or different personae. Part of your set design could include a hat rack with hats, feather boas, scarves, or jackets that are worn at times and replaced on the rack when not in use.

Other production concepts might call for a performing group to have ensemble dress. This could be merely the same color or identical unisex color-coordinated outfits. For a production centered on the health professions, the cast members may all wear the ubiquitous white jackets worn by doctors or hospital orderlies. For a production centered on the value and legacy of the farmer, all cast members might wear overalls with bib straps. The theme and focus of any production should provide clues for optional ensemble dress.

Lighting and Media Usage

Lighting may or may not be factored into the production. It certainly can focus attention on varying areas for performance, produce atmosphere and dramatic effect, be used for slides or other projected imagery, and signal scene transitions. Some Readers Theatre productions have used rear projection lighting through translucent scrims to suggest silhouettes.

Media can enhance Readers Theatre productions. Music can be live, accompanied with instruments left on stage. Singing can be a cappella (without instruments, only vocal) or augmented by musical accompaniment (e.g., guitar or flute). If singing is to be done, make sure that all cast members can harmonize or at least match the same pitch on the melodies.

Other mixed-media devices used in Readers Theatre productions include: vocal sound effects, electronic sounds (e.g., percussive beats from keyboards, tape recorders, or metronomes), artwork, magic tricks, dance, and voiceovers/recordings superimposed on the live production. Take care that the media inclusions do not usurp the focus on the text in performance. "Special effects" cannot be the only memory and use of imagination by an observing audience.

Conclusion

In Chapter 9 you will be introduced to the concept of creating a production guide. This guide will include not only the performance script but explanations and design elements for the staging of the production.

You will be asked to diagram a playing area with set pieces and show transitional movements from one scene or episode to another. Some directors block only after gathering all the cast members for a rehearsal, recording the choices and decisions as variable positions and movements are considered. To be considerate to any and all casts, directors need to come to staging and blocking rehearsals with some design concept in mind. Whether you draw out envisioned graphics of scene movement or freely "block as you go," all directors should be open to cast suggestions for movement and blocking. The final decision must be always in the hands of a director, but all shows have varying degrees of alteration in blocking from initial placements.

In some texts, a director may choose to block movements backwards to consider "how do we get to this formation" from another stage picture. Cast members need to be patient with blocking and movement rehearsals, allowing for "trial and error" and "experimentation." A director should not exasperate his/her cast with indecision, but quickly embrace a movement concept and design perspective. In Chapter 8 we will investigate the "creative" notions for Readers Theatre productions, capitalizing on the various means to let creativity generate nuances in production staging and conceptualizations. One closing note is necessary: Movement for movement's sake is unnecessary and distracting, but a production without key movement decisions tends to be boring and uninteresting; let the creative "juices" flow as you determine how a production will unfold its staging concepts.

Discussion and Assignments

1. Assign to a two- to three-person group a project to assemble a small box or platform with plywood that is painted black. Make the boxes or platforms varying heights and available for class use for any assigned performances later in the quarter or semester.

2. Take time during class to demonstrate varying stage movements along the "x," "y," and "z" axis. Choose shorter and taller members of the class and discuss ways to stage clusters without hiding anyone. Place four or five members on a straight line facing the audience and ask the audience if they perceive this formation as boring. Why? Are there any dangers or drawbacks to certain staging setups? How would you make stage pictures safer? What makes stage pictures more interesting to an audience member?

3. Does a performing cast resent a director who has no preconceived blocking ideas or should most casts be willing to spend extra rehearsals in experimentation with blocking?

4. Solve this problem: The director wants to add a cappella singing to the transitions for the production. Of the five cast members all four can stay on pitch but one cast member is definitely not a singer and cannot match the pitch. How do you include the singing, but not let the one performer ruin the musical interlude? How do you prevent the perception of the obvious exclusion of one performer in the singing portions?

5. For the small cast show of two or three performers, discuss and describe various blocking movements, stage pictures, and cluster options. What will you do as a director to keep audience interest in the movements and stage pictures of such a small cast show?

6. For a large cast show of six to eight or more performers, discuss and describe various blocking movements, stage pictures, and cluster options. What do you do with cast members who are out of the scene, yet cannot exit the playing area? Where will you place them and what might you have them do if you desire to keep them in a scene, but not delivering lines?

References

1. Joanna Hawkins Maclay, *Readers Theatre: Toward a Grammar of Practice* (New York: Random House, 1971), 45.

2. Maclay, *Readers Theatre*, 35.

3. Liesel Reinhart, Personal interview, April 21, 2006.

8

Creativity in Textual Performances

Richard Dean Anderson is a well-recognized television actor, having recently starred in the syndicated science fiction series, *Stargate SG-1*. But Anderson is probably even more well known as a historical television "icon" for his late 1980s/early 1990s portrayal of a man who was never at a loss for discovering unpredictable means to escape danger and doom in his role on the television show, *MacGyver*. (Anderson even revived the MacGyver character in a 2006 MasterCard commercial.) MacGyver could take objects and use them in nonpredictable ways. He was a man who could think creatively and not succumb to "set" thinking.

Set thinking is the normal realm for most human beings and when you discover someone who can think "outside the box," you find yourself amazed. This particular chapter will be less formal, more personal than any other chapter in this text because it relies on recollections and interactions with the myriad of "creative" people I have met in my life over the years of writing and directing Readers Theatre presentations who could create visions for performance in ways that denied set thinking. I have found no other Readers Theatre text that has offered a chapter in notions of creative thinking for theatrical vision and design, so this chapter will hopefully be a unique opportunity to allow you also to think "outside of the box."

To begin this creative quest, I would like to return to an amplified quotation I referenced earlier in this text from Michael G. Leigh:

> Free-association is the crucible of most creativity. One sees two or more things not previously seen in connection with each other and one draws them together, like rock and roll and a bag lady, into the cross-pollination of the imagination....I suspect that most people free-associate some fairly wonderful creative ideas. As they say, everyone has one novel in them. I suspect that everyone has a couple of readers theatre scripts in them, but most don't trust that unconscious process which is the beginning of all creations, the void from which there is light. Confessedly, it takes some nerve to turn one's fantasies inside-out for the world. But the daring to do so is so cathartic, it's worth the chance. It's fun.[1]

It is fun. It is also especially energizing to catch the vision of an idea that uses texts, set pieces, props, and unexpected additional staging devices in nonpredictable ways.

Creativity in Finding and Selecting Texts

Most Readers Theatre adaptor/directors begin the creative process with finding the most intriguing texts. Liesel Reinhart of Mount San Antonio College represents most RT adaptor/directors when she shares that

> I do a lot of reading. Sometimes I just read jackets of books or the first few paragraphs of an article, sometimes I read whole novels or plays. Occasionally a piece of music or a film will get an idea going, but more often than not it's a written or oral text for me. I also get a lot of ideas from students. They are often exposed

to different kinds of texts than I am, like weblogs, for instance. In general, I think everyone involved in the creative process of writing the RT needs to be open and looking for topic ideas over a period of time. It is very difficult to go out in a single afternoon and say, "I will find a good theatre idea today."[2]

Sometimes the creative spark sets off a chain of events that begins with a key text, but leads to other similar or contrasting texts. You must guard against redundancy in texts if you collect text samples in this manner. Still, "when you start to assemble texts that capture the feeling or essence of the other materials, you have a better chance of creating a piece with more overall integrity."[3] Beginning with a word or a topic is only the beginning of this creativity in collecting texts. A focusing process will occur that will narrow the word or topic to a thesis or argument or communicative center, the rhetorical perspective that has been mentioned many times already in this text.

I am a firm believer in the collection of materials and text portions and placing them in folders for later use. I may read a text and think, "That has possibilities for a Readers Theatre show" and make a copy of it and file it away. Some production adaptors/directors begin with the key text and look for comparative and contrasting texts to "spoke out" from that core text. Intertexuality encourages this association concept and expects that new ideas about a theme or message will result. The link to new concepts does not always come from literary or even "oral" texts either. I found a psychological/sociological journal article that articulated a hierarchy of stress-filled activities that provided the structure for a Readers Theatre program on stress. I merely found texts to illustrate each of the hierarchical activities, culminating in the most stressful event: loss of a spouse or a child.

Creativity cannot be forced, however. Famous writers and producers get "writer's block" and must step away from their in-process work to refresh their minds and hopefully clear the obstacles to creative thought. Creativity is probably never completely the ability to bring into existence something out of nothing either. (For those who believe in God, the "Creator" aspects are relegated to the Diety, but most religions acknowledge that this Diety has infused followers with a "creative spark" that emulates the Divine, but now in human endeavors.)

Creativity in the Production Vision

How do we learn to let our creative "juices" flow and find fruition in production visions? I believe we get the "spark" going by observing others who observed others who observed others. The creative vision frequently owes much to observation and new applications.

Over the years I have learned so much and attempted new creative approaches from watching the productions of my colleagues. (I certainly benefited from watching the brilliant and creative Readers Theatre productions produced and directed by many, many others, especially those I have listed in the preface.) In 2001, I was asked to be on a panel of critics for the initial national tournament/conference for the American Readers Theatre Association (ARTa) at Mount San Antonio College in Walnut, California. I share my experiences of being overwhelmed by the creativity of one group production entitled "Guernica," starring four performers from Mount San Antonio College, the host school. The title comes from a painting by Pablo Picasso and this Readers Theatre production won several awards at this inaugural national tournament.[4] I was overwhelmed by not only the notion that poetry, nonfiction, and documentary materials could be woven into a collage program that was so biographical, yet universal in thematic application, I was overcome by the creativity expressed in this production. Individual set pieces were long, slender wooden planks that when turned around at the end of the program came together to form the actual reproduction of the Guernica painting by Picasso. The various set pieces were incorporated into every aspect of the production, but only seen as a "gestalt" of the original painting at the conclusion.

The creative forces behind this production and so many others that I have witnessed began with the notion that *set thinking must be minimized*. Set thinking looks at a block or even text options and says, "This can only be used, produced, or performed in one way." Creative people look at possibilities and say, "This could be something other than what it appears to be."

You might have seen the brilliant improvisational television show hosted by Drew Carey called *Whose Line Is It Anyway?* A recurring bit on that show had the gifted comics given unusual or even obvious props or what we might label as "set pieces." The segment asked these performers to improvise a scene with the object with a seemingly brief period of preparation time. So a road warning cone becomes a hearing aide, a witch hat, and a megaphone. Creative Readers Theatre performers can do this with set pieces or props as well, but the end goal should never be to dazzle an audience with the nifty trick for the sake of itself and the "oooh and ahhhhh" reaction from the audience. Any creativity used should always link the non-set thinking to a meaningful way to present a text.

I had a production I directed several years ago that needed a long platform, about 2 feet off the ground and about 7 feet long, where performers could sit as well as stand on the piece. This set piece was not extremely heavy, but awkward enough that two performers were needed at all times to move it to the performance arena. I figured that it would merely be stationary throughout the entire production. Since the production was a compiled script, I came to a place in the creative process where I was stumped. I had a comic scene later on that needed something else with a set background and I could not figure out how to move beyond set thinking to work out the problem. One afternoon, prior to the cast meeting me in rehearsal, I was alone in the practice room staring at that long platform and wondering if it could help me with my comic scene problem. I thought, "Why does that platform have to be only used as something on which to sit or stand? Why couldn't it be stood on end, turned around and transformed into a telephone booth for this comic scene?" The second notion for creativity practice was exercised: *When facing an obstacle, improvise alternatives for a solution.* Tipping up the platform and having a performer stand in front of it with a mimed telephone conversation to another part of the playing area created a moment of behavioral synecdoche (remember Chapter 2!) that "created" the illusion for the audience. The creative spark originated from frustration and a desire to consider alternative solutions to overcome an obstacle.

Many of my friends and colleagues have told me that they wake up sometimes in the middle of the night, having dreamed of an answer to a staging dilemma and realizing that if they did not write it down or draw a picture it would evaporate. Others have determined that the answer to the problems faced needed other options and thus many new productions have moved away from dependence on blocks, platforms, or ladders to the inclusion of reams of fabric for set design and nuanced suggestions. Set pieces may now be built as elaborate parts of a "jigsaw puzzle" that come together in other portions of the production to take on new usages. "Creativity frequently happens because of a need and of a conscious process of thinking how to come up with a different solution than the expected."[5]

The third notion for operationalizing creativity is: *Suspend critical judgment.* Never assume that because something has never been attempted that it cannot find a way to work. I had a production that needed a percussive and repetitive drumbeat to sustain a rap or chantlike version of a popular rock-and-roll song. This repetitive beat kept the cast on the rhythm of the piece because without it we found ourselves losing the "beat." I could not find a keyboardist with an instrument to take with us to tournament competition (nor could I find anyone who was available to perform the RT plus play the instrument) so I recorded the track on a simple cassette (I know this dates me...) and placed a boom box (remember those?) under a platform and pushed play and stop for the duration of this introduction. I suspended the judgment of how to solve the problem until I considered as many possibilities as I could imagine. The rhythm portion worked and perhaps I helped influence others as so many have influenced me.

144

There must always be a "freedom to try" when facing your production obstacles. Several adaptors/directors will establish extended rehearsals to incorporate the "freedom to try" principle; various optional movements will be attempted until one will be chosen that seems to work efficiently. The "freedom to try" concept also works for textual choices as well. Sometimes the best solution to a problem of text is to creatively compose a text of your own. Original material can be linked to your own name or if you prefer anonymity, use a pen name. Even though a script may go through the entire pre-production process with texts in place, once you attempt to creatively bring the production to life you may need to substitute or delete texts in favor of other ones you discover along the production process way.

A fourth notion about creativity is: *provide opportunities to associate new concepts together.* Blocking ideas frequently do not originate with the adaptor/director, but come from the cast members. You could allow the cast members to play a scene and improvise their locations and distance and interactions. The result is frequently not what a director had in mind, but could be quite useful and necessary to maintain in the production vision. Giving cast members the opportunity to associate new concepts together, even in basic blocking, can assist the cast in learning to "own" the show as their own as well. A single stool with a revolving seat could be associated as a "merry-go-round" if a cast member sits on it, but the remainder of the cast grabs onto a string or fabric that can simulate the object. In this example, the merry-go-round illusion is a new concept, developed from the basic concept of a revolving stool.

Notions That Foster Creativity
1. Set thinking must be minimized.
2. When facing an obstacle, improvise alternatives for a solution.
3. Suspend critical judgment.
4. Provide opportunities to associate new concepts together.
5. Think like *MacGyver*.

Figure 8.1

I believe I can summarize the notions that foster creativity by remind-
ing us all to *think like MacGyver*. As we are so often reminded, the hair
pins, the shaving cream, the paper clip, the spool of wire, and the pair
of tube socks used by MacGyver to exit a burning building all have
associations and uses apart from how *he* used each item. But thinking
outside of that which is predictable truly is wonderful and exhilarating.
Watching other artists, not merely to copy or reproduce their work,
should inspire us to try something new or explore the undeveloped
options for new associations. Everyone indeed does have something
creative waiting to be unleashed and one of the best outlets is a Readers
Theatre production.

Discussion and Assignments

1. Spend class time working in a group activity with the creativity exercise found in the Appendix. Set up your available set pieces and have members involved in this exercise demonstrate optional means to block or create a stage picture with suggestions from the artistic fields of cinema, conventional theatre, literary analysis, and other media formats. Write down your observations and find a way to incorporate some of these creative notions into your own production.

2. Listen to any kind of music that has an inherent story. Invite a discussion as to how you might creatively design a production with just the text being presented without the music.

3. The ancient Greeks developed their myths mainly through contests that are historical antecedents to modern-day forensics contests. A gifted storyteller would begin a story and end it with a cliff hanger portion and another storyteller would pick up and continue the story. Break into groups of at least five or six and begin a story, then creatively pick up the thread of the story and embellish it before passing it on to the next member of the group. How does creativity play out when you must pick up a story and then leave it dangling for someone else to finish? Who would win the contest for creative storytelling in your group? Why?

References

1. Michael G. Leigh, *The Care and Feeding of Readers Theatre: A Manual for Instructors and Directors.* (Privately published and copyrighted by Michael G. Leigh: 1991), 27.

2. Liesel Reinhart, Personal interview, April 21, 2006.

3. Reinhart interview.

4. The Audience Award, the Outstanding Achievement in Script, the Outstanding Achievement in Set, the Special Award for Thematic Excellence, the Special Award for Creative Innovation, and the Overall Champion Award were all won by this production.

5. Liana Koeppel-Taylor, Personal interview, March 20, 2006.

9

Preparing the Production Guide/Script; Rehearsals in Preparation for Performance

With each new Readers Theatre production, the preproduction preparation will become easier and capable of being accomplished with minimal written work. But since this is probably your first attempt to assemble a group performance of literature text and commentary, you need to create a *production guide* for your assistance as well as for your cast of performers.

Any production guide consists of two parts: (1) the guide itself, and (2) the actual formatted performable script. You may choose to adapt any form of literature or "oral" text as a "single" selection or a "compiled/collage" program. For class purposes you will be asked to create a script that has a performance time of between 15 and 25 minutes as directed by your instructor.

Production Guide Essentials

You can format your typed responses to fit an 8 ½ by 11 inch notebook (utilizing standard-size printer paper). However, you may wish to reformat the guide's essential information to fit a 7 by 9 inch three-ring binder notebook if the actual scripted text fits that size. Every production guide should include the following topics, labeled and amplified by insightful commentary, in the given order:

1. *Theme/Rhetorical Statement/Overview*: Write at least one paragraph describing the primary theme of the texts you use in the script. If you have contrasting multiple texts, write a second paragraph describing the aspects of the primary theme that will be performed, commenting on the order of the texts and how the progression of theme development unfolds in performance. In a third paragraph, reference the analytical perspectives that will promote this production concept. In other words, state a *rhetorical thesis sentence* and how each text supports or contrasts your analytical performance choices. Finally, write out the titles of each text (or episodes in a single text) with the label "transition" for connecting statements you will use in a listing. Provide the total number of your cast and which gender will perform each numbered part.

2. *Work Units/"Scene" Divisions*: Divide the performance script into motivational working units for study and rehearsals. Answer this question: Why have you divided the script this way and into these working units? Keep the segments short enough (1 to 1½ pages) to aid rehearsal periods. You should separate these "scenes" in your typed script copy by a series of hyphens or a centered underline mark of 10 to 15 connected separation symbols (e.g., ********** or +++++++++++ or _____). In this part of the production guide indicate the total number of working units you have established in the actual text. Within the actual performance script you should label each of these segments as "Scene One, Scene Two, etc.".

3. *Description of Characters/Performers*: Provide an overall perspective on performer challenges as identified by performer number. Begin with Performer 1 and systematically describe each character, narrator, or persona that this performer will offer. Summarize briefly but include more than one paragraph

per performer if necessary. Comment on attitude, demeanor, and vocal changes for each persona presented by an individual performer. Add analytical commentary about desired perspective for each persona offered by this performer. Do the same for each performer. Each descriptive paragraph begins with "Performer 1 plays these characters...; Performer Two plays these characters...; etc.".

4. **Focus:** Describe the type of focus used in each scene. Indicate where performers should place their eye gaze in order to be consistent with the focal choice. State why and for what purpose a focal choice is made for each individual work unit or scene.

5. **Blocking/Movement/Set Pieces:** The bulk of this portion of your production guide will consist of a scale drawing of the initial set design and location as well as changes or alterations in the performing area as scenes change. Summarize the size, shape, and color of your set pieces. Scene 1 will be the default position and draw pictures to indicate people and objects. Use geometric shapes or pictures to establish different boxes, platforms, or set pieces. Use squares, rectangles, triangles, circles, and oblongs with a "code breaker" somewhere on your drawing page. This usually appears at the bottom (e.g., ▼ = "stool," ■ = "platform," ■ = "small box," etc.). Identify performers by number or letter and draw arrows to where you want them to move and when this should occur. Write out descriptions of movements in a paragraph, excerpting lines per scene and use a different color pen or ink to indicate the move on your graphic chart. Say, "1 moves on. . . ," then state the portion of the line that begins the movement. Use stage direction commentary to identify direction for your movements. Indicate how each performer will enter or exit the scene and what entrance/exit device will be used to signal this in the scene. Do this for each scene or work unit. A ten scene performance script will need at least six or seven diagrammed blocking/ movement portions (and probably a few more if you move within a scene frequently).

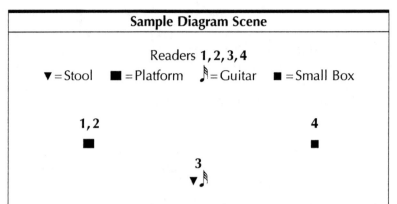

Stage Directions: 1 and 2 mount the platform box on first words of the scene; 3 sits down on the stool, picks up guitar, begins to sing; 4 stands on the small box and delivers narrative line after the first verse of the song.

Figure 9.1

6. ***Costuming/Presence or Absence of Script/Lighting and Media:*** In a paragraph describe individual performer costume needs or the ensemble color choices and dress designs. If you have a hat rack with added costume features, describe these additions and in what work units they are needed. If scripts are to be used, indicate the color and design of the three-ring binder notebook. If scripts are to be used as props, identify by each scene how and why "script as prop" should occur. If scripts are not be used or used at minimal specified times, indicate what performers should do with body language, presentational aspects, focal points, as well as where they might pick up scripts for later use and reference while the presentation is ongoing. If lighting is to be used, identify in each scene the desired kind of lighting, spotlight usage, or projection effect. If media is used, indicate where it will be used in relation to the set design and stage properties. For example, if a live instrument (e.g., guitar)

is to be a part of the set design for some scene uses, establish a symbolic code for the guitar and its stand (e.g., ♪ = instrument).

You may wish to include director commentary in each segment of the guide. This can incorporate your analytical interpretations of the texts. Have this plan available for your rehearsals, but be flexible to change aspects that do not seem to work. It is true that the rehearsal process will probably alter the imagined production guide choices based on observation and practice. However, avoid too many comments as a director such as "We'll figure out how to block this when we get to rehearsals." Casts will have greater faith and respect in directors who truly have worked to design and articulate their production vision.

Actual Script

The actual script should be typed and formatted to 8½ by 11 inches (or to 6½ by 8½ inches for inclusion in 7 by 9 inch three-ring binder notebooks). Double-spacing makes it easier to read (if the script is to be present) as does a font size of 10 or 12. Do not type up performance script with an exotic font style; stay with fonts like the ones found in textbooks or formal journal articles. Set off performer numbers (numbers only) to the far left, use a colon, then indent to begin the line. Allow enough room on both left and right margins for the three-hole positions to fit into the notebook used. Format the lines so that they are automatically indented underneath the preceding line, not the performer number. Type so that any performer has a complete segment on one page, not stuck turning a page in the middle of a sentence or thought group (whenever possible). If you type a performer's lines over to the next page, there is the possibility of creating a difficult or awkward connection, pausing in mid-section or mid-thought unnecessarily.

Every segment, scene, or work unit should be labeled as "Scene One, Scene Two, etc." You may desire to handwrite in the scene number and labels at a later time or type them in as desired.

The script should be checked for spelling and grammatical errors and corrections made. The copy in the production guide should be printed with enough clarity to be xeroxed. Computer printed copies require legibility for all performers as well as the director.

It is difficult to estimate the time length of a production script based on page numbers. If typing a normal 8½ by 11 inch page, you should have 18 to 24 pages typed, indented, double-spaced equal 20 to 25 minutes in performance time. If after initial rehearsals the script is running too long, you will need to delete or edit lines and possibly retype the script for the performers. A script that is too short may need additional pages, identified on a temporary basis by subset "a, b, c" (e.g., Page 3a, 3b, 3c, preceding Page 4).

Doing a complete production guide is tedious work, but having it in a director's hand will enhance the rehearsal process. Your instructor will indicate when your production guide will be due. This is such an important part of the class requirements that many instructors will not accept late production guides. Many instructors choose class performance assignments based on their reading and assessments of individualized production guides. Most classes set aside time until the end of the semester for in-class rehearsals, pointing toward the actual performance for class and invited audience members. With a production guide and the script in hand, it is now time to turn to rehearsals.

Auditioning

If your production guide and script is chosen for classroom performance, you may be required to cast other class members in the parts. Outside of class you may be inclined to cast performers for certain parts based on a small circle of friends or acquaintances. I recommend a wider search whenever possible. Announce auditions for your planned performance. You may even decide to precede the actual audition with a survey card, which indicates interest, age level, availability, and experience. But once you establish a time for an audition, consider reproducing this sample audition "card:" (See Figure 9.2)

AUDITION INFORMATION FOR: (Name of the Show Here)

Name:_____

Telephone/Cell Number: _____

Address: _____

City: _____

E-mail Address: _____

Year in School:_____

Briefly summarize your RT or acting experience/list shows and years:

Rehearsals will be Tuesday, Wednesday, Thursday nights from 6:30 until 9:30 P.M. beginning on _____; List any times you cannot make rehearsals:

You must be available during preview/dress rehearsal week for every night; you must be available to help load as well as take down the set (if necessary). Performances will be:

Figure 9.2

You should ask those who come to an audition time period to bring or prepare the following:

1. A memorized 1 to 2 minute monologue for presentation.

2. If musical assessment is needed, a ten-bar sample of singing, accompanied or a cappella (Bring your own sheet music).

3. A schedule of free time when not in class or working a job (in case pickup rehearsals are necessary)

In addition, you may audition individually or in small groups, providing one page from the performance text to be read "cold." Provide different portions of the performance script so as to get a sense of performance ability in a variety of parts. If you have too many people to audition, narrow the field to offer a "call back" audition and let the results determine your casting decision.

Do not destroy the audition cards because sometimes the individuals you cast may drop out and you may need to make substitution decisions. Make it clear to all performers about the expectations and the dedication required to the rehearsal and performance process. Choose those who not only exhibit ranges in vocal tone, credibility, pitch and vocal skill variety, and enthusiasm, but also the somewhat enigmatic but powerful concept of "stage presence."

Rehearsals

The first two rehearsals should consist of the distribution of performance scripts and "cold readings" through the entire script. Have several participants read for a director, changing to different parts until the best match emerges. It may be necessary to change numbered parts once rehearsals begin to comprise different or switched portions. It is always easier to adapt to your cast than to try and force someone to perform only the originally designed performer designations.

At the time of the third to fifth rehearsal, the director should begin to foster dialogue about the production concept or vision. Ratliff suggests that in these early rehearsals one should "indicate the literary character's emotional or intellectual condition and reveal the chronological or sequential events revealed in the story line."[1] Some directors ask performers to write out character analysis descriptions. Other directors ask probing questions about possible back story or motivations not apparent in the performance script. It is quite possible that a director will have to tell cast members about important details and information cut or deleted from earlier versions of the script, but essential for choices in performance. These early rehearsals need to allow time for discussion and dialogue about the production concept. Everyone in the cast needs to know how each one fits into the presentation of the rhetorical message. Directors do have the final say about interpretation and intent, but should be open to changes if cast members have a viable alternative to offer.

Depending on the experience level of the cast, directors may need to read a line to demonstrate a desired choice. Good directors give very clear advice and must find a balance between showing a performer what is expected and letting a performer "grow" in the part with his/her own demonstrated choices. Generally, most performers will seem more willing to work and spend the time periods going over sections if a director offers constructive criticism, credible choices, and affirms performer discoveries.

The middle rehearsals do not have a precise number but should be established by a schedule of scenes to be covered. Ask cast members to bring their scripts and pencils for writing down notes to each rehearsal. These middle rehearsals need to emphasize not only line interpretations, but energetic cue pickups, consistent phrasing rhythm, matching voices in the harmonies of choral recitation, consistent focal points, timing, and credible personae choices.

You can begin staging and blocking arrangements during these middle rehearsals also. Have the cast members write down movements and stage directions in the script margins. If the staging and movement conceptualized in the production guide is not working, modify or alter the movement so it does work. Some directors increase the number and length of these movement rehearsals so as to experience viable decisions based on cast suggestions or trial and error. Later rehearsals at this stage need to clearly emphasize off-the-script familiarity or complete memorization.

Whenever possible have at least two "dress" rehearsals. Have the cast wear their costumes or ensemble dress. Invite a small select audience of friends to come to both rehearsals. Remember that when an audience laughs, you must hold the next line delivery until the laughter subsides. Be ready for something to go wrong because it frequently does. Learn to keep going and not break character. Pick up a cue or a line, covering for another's mistakes or omissions. If any minor adjustments need to be made, try them out at the end of these dress rehearsals in your cast meeting.

And now the day has arrived for the first "real" performance. Whether in a classroom or on a stage platform, let the nervous energy connect with an interested audience and allow the interactive process to commence. Hopefully, this will not be a once only performance. Nevertheless, let each performance share the rhetorical themes and the compelling messages found in the vast array of literary and "oral" traditions.

Discussion and Assignments

1. Your instructor will remind you of the date when the production guide and script will be due in class. He/she will return your guides and indicate which ones have been chosen for classroom presentation. The remainder of the course schedule will include in-class rehearsal time and a final performance date and time as well.

2. Why is it important for a director to affirm performers, commenting on what was done well as well as offering constructive criticism for improvement? What happens to cast members if they only hear critical or negative or no feedback from their rehearsal process?

3. How does a director solve the problem of a cast that sounds "too rehearsed" (i.e., each line sounds memorized with little feeling or spontaneity)?

4. Once a script has been approved with all of the minor changes and corrections, some performers like to highlight their own lines with a yellow marker or some other color for highlighting/underlining. Does this device have any merit at all—or is it distracting?

5. Directors should investigate the use of "warm-up theatre exercises" prior to the dress and actual performances. How do these "game activities" prepare a cast for the actual performance?

6. For in-class performances, your instructor may ask all of the participants to tear out the evaluation form from the Appendix and do peer-grading of the director, providing constructive commentary about their experience as cast members. The director will also fill out evaluation forms on the participants, providing a peer-grading that will be considered by the

instructor for the overall project grade. For those in the audience or perhaps for the instructor, fill out the overall RT evaluation sheet and provide copies to all involved in the production.

References

1. Gerald Lee Ratliff, *Introduction to Readers Theatre: A Guide to Classroom Performance* (Colorado Springs, CO: Meriwether Publishing Ltd., 1999), 20.

10

Outlets for Readers Theatre Performance

There is most definitely an audience for Readers Theatre presentations outside of the classroom. In fact, there are many audiences, drawn together by interests or circumstances that will appreciate the creativity and message-centered approach of this group performance format.

As you consider future options for RT performance venues, you could naturally begin on your own campus. Organize an evening or two of class productions and invite the general public to attend. Found space on your campus may be varied, may be indoors or outside, may be an intimate black box theatre or a massive proscenium auditorium. It does not matter where the found space is as long as an audience can discover the location and the excitement for theatrical creativity that awaits them.

Your campus venues are only the beginning for Readers Theatre outlets for performance. In this final chapter you will discover options that include: forensics/festivals, children's groups, religious centers, wedding ceremonies, and social services.

Forensics and Festivals

Academic cocurricular communication competition is labeled as *forensics* (a term connected to ancient Greek legal communication and since the early 1900s applied to argumentative educational debate and public address contests). Since the early 1970s, forensics competition expanded to include oral interpretation and Readers Theatre competition.

Community colleges have assumed the primary lead in introducing Readers Theatre competition in local, regional, state, and national tournaments. Phi Rho Pi, the community college forensics association, has Readers Theatre as a popular component of its spring national tournament each year. But four-year colleges and universities have begun to participate in RT as well. Leagues and restricted collegiate tournaments, open to league members from all level colleges, regularly offer a group performance of literature event.

The largest forensics-type group performance competition for all schools is sponsored by ARTa, the American Readers Theatre Association. ARTa began in 2001 through funding and support from Mount San Antonio College in Walnut, California. This Southern California location has seen incredible innovations and creativity in the art form. An estimated twenty or more troupes from various states travel to the campus in May of each year. Awards and honors go to: the Champion Team; Audience Favorite; World Premiere (the first presentation of the script is at this event); Outstanding Ensemble Cast; Outstanding Male and Female Performers; Achievements in Script, Costuming, Set, and Blocking; and special awards for Thematic Excellence and Creative Innovation. Any college can pay a subscriber/ entrance fee and enter the competition. (See contact information at the end of this chapter.)

Festivals for solo and group performance of literature join seminars about the art form with noncompetitive classroom encounters with guest academic critics. (ARTa also includes a pretournament semi-

164

nar/workshop day as well.) Formats differ throughout the United States and Canada, but normally a group performs for a panel of academic critics and a reaction and response dialogue ensues after the performance. Comments center on appreciation and analysis of the performance. The focus of the festival environment is not competitive, but endorses learning, development of skills and insights, and especially dialogue. Festivals are quite casual and less threatening by design. Festivals usually take place over a two- or three-day weekend.[1]

In both forensics tournaments and festivals, group presentations require multiple performances, usually three at a minimum. The found space is the classroom, but final performances move to larger performing arenas to accommodate expansive crowds. Each outlet may have rules or expectations (e.g., time limits) to make the activity feasible and efficient. Both festivals and forensics tournaments have educational values. Both need to be supported and endorsed by educators from varying perspectives.

Children's Groups

Local elementary schools (and some middle schools) love to have collegiate group performance troupes come and offer classroom as well as all-school assemblies. The challenges for the performers lie primarily in text selection and maintaining audience interest.

Text selection must anticipate the grade levels in the audience. Finding texts that give vent to a child's imagination are paramount. Texts should provide opportunities for wonder, laughter, action, excitement, and sometimes audience interaction and involvement. Length of time cannot exceed 15 or 20 minutes in most cases. Attention spans at this level are fairly short. Try to find texts with repetition of sounds and actions, vivid imagery, fun rhyming words, and plotlines of familiar tensions for kids.

For example, Liana Koeppel-Taylor, professor of speech at Cypress College in Cypress, California, regularly compiles and adapts programs designed for elementary school assemblies and presented by her collegiate students:

> I'm doing Readers Theatre both with performing *for* children and also *using* children. I've done a lot of programs with the kids themselves....The difficulty with doing Readers Theatre for children is the broad age range. What is appealing to a kindergartner and what's appealing to a fifth grader can be difficult. We aimed for the middle...with Dr. Seuss' *Horton Hears a Who*....But we put in humor that the older kids will appreciate....They really respond to Readers Theatre.... We also get one of the teachers to do a little part, a surprise. And the kids love that![2]

Subtlety is usually too complex for young children, so giving vent to uninhibited performance choices probably works best. Kids love enthusiastic performers. They love distinct character voices with funny inflections and gestures. Koeppel-Taylor indicates that "we added in a character with the line 'I'll be back!' with an Arnold [Schwarzeneggar] voice and the older kids got it and laughed."[3]

To find suitable children's literature, visit your public library or a nearby bookstore. Re-discover (or maybe "discover" for the first time) the humorous worlds of Norton Juster (*The Phantom Tollbooth*), Judith Viorst (*Alexander and the Terrible, Horrible, No Good, Very Bad Day*), Roald Dahl (*Charlie and the Chocolate Factory; The Twits*), Shel Silverstein (poems plus *The Giving Tree*), Dr. Seuss, C. S. Lewis, The Brothers Grimm, and so many others.

Religious Centers

Fear of mixing church and state in public education creates an aversion to studying the Bible as literature occasionally, but the performance of religious scriptures or religious stories does not need to be sectarian. Religious scriptures are filled with great prose and poetry selections, epic tales, stirring imagery, and deep philosophical ponderings.

Readers Theatre techniques can, however, add to the sense and devotion of a worship experience. A Catholic Mass has routinized the traditional call and response of formal liturgy between priest and congregational member. I recall being intrigued by my visit to Temple Beth Tikvah, a Reformed Jewish synagogue in Columbus, Ohio, and hearing a traditional Jewish liturgical service divided into lines between selected readers on microphones and those worshippers attending the service. The scripts were handed out as people entered the synagogue and the format was genuine Readers Theatre.

In some churches a Readers Theatre-type scene, lasting perhaps a maximum of five minutes, coincides with the sermon topic and serves a smiliar purpose to "special music." Some religious publishers provide original essays and texts for Readers Theatre presentations.[4] Sometimes the biblical text for the day is divided into portions for individual and group recitations. Choral reading of scripture alternates with a lay leader who serves as the primary reader/performer.

Some other religious worship centers could reformat traditional approaches to group presentation. The *Mahabharata* is a two-thousand-year-old Indian poem and serves as the basis for Hindu religion, history, and philosophy. Composed of one hundred Sanskrit couplets, this massive work has several English translations and narrative elements with dialogue suitable for presentation by a group. The *Qu'ran*, the holy book of Islam, also has narratives and pronouncements that could be presented in an effective oral presentation format.

All too often those who present religious texts forget that they are rich in characterization, passion, nuance, rhythm, and vivid imagery. Prepare and present the world's religious literature with the same attention to "drama" as any other text.

Wedding Ceremonies

My wife and I incorporated a brief Readers Theatre program into our wedding service. I wrote the script, including details of our past, how we met, and our future dreams. My former students agreed to be the performers and the inclusion was received well by all in attendance. Many said, "I've never seen anything like that at a wedding before."

Today's weddings have the ubiquitous "slide show" as part of the service or during the reception period. A Readers Theatre "program" could accompany the slide show or stand alone. Some wedding services ask for the "witnesses" to acknowledge support for the blissful couple and a Readers Theatre interactive program, distributed along with the wedding program, could provide a significant symbolic presentation of vows as well as supportive involvement by those guests in attendance.

Social Services

Unions, political parties, consumer groups, and social awareness committees can make use of Readers Theatre to offer alternative proposals and set up the potential for attitude as well as behavioral change. These groups usually have persuasive messages to share and RT-type presentations use drama to get attention as well as results.

Libraries are no longer merely book repositories. Most libraries now offer a myriad of services for online research as well as community meeting places. Most libraries (and now even some fancy bookstores) sponsor reading hours. Even without normal staging areas available,

Readers Theatre can adapt to any found space and becomes an ideal format to raise consciousness and encourage the reading of library books.

Service clubs are constantly on the lookout for free or minimal cost programs. Kiwanis, Rotary, Lions, and Sertoma clubs would welcome a seasonal Readers Theatre program or a program intended to raise social consciousness. Since these service clubs normally meet over a meal in restaurants or recreational facilities, the found space can be created by merely pushing back a few tables and chairs to create a playing arena, visible to all in attendance.

Senior assisted-living homes appreciate thoughtful programs brought to them in their dining halls or television rooms. The inability to travel to a local theatre is overcome when a Readers Theatre troupe comes to a senior home. Programs should be brief for seniors as their attention span may have dwindled over the years. Readers Theatre presentations frequently serve more than an entertainment purpose. RT can help promote therapy for the aged and the handicapped (even the blind and the deaf). Those who are blind will find it easy to understand the text-focused aspects of Readers Theatre. Those who are deaf could read lips or follow the staging with key elements written out on poster boards and incorporated into a production. Young people who are also in assisted care due to catastrophic illnesses will appreciate a Readers Theatre production performed within the confines of their otherwise somber hospital room or gathering locale.

Conclusion

There seemingly is no end to the potential outlets for service and impact when Readers Theatre productions are made viable and mobile. And the experiences you gain from participating as a performer as well as adaptor/director will make you a more effective communicator (and person!) no matter what vocation you choose.

Whatever outlets you pursue, remember that you bring to each new encounter a legacy of oral tradition, confidence, and sensitivity. Presentational performance reminds you continually of the power of theatre as persuasive message. You will be able to continually tap into the experienced skills of poise, energy, and dramatic enthusiasm no matter what you do in life. Each group performance of literature experience provides the means to explore a universe of thought, philosophy, and human values. Readers Theatre has a rich heritage and you will reap benefits because of your involvement in this wonderful activity for the rest of your life.

Discussion and Assignments

1. If you have a potential Readers Theatre program ready to be presented at the American Readers Theatre Association annual conference and tournament in May, ask your instructor to ask for details and payment instructions at this address: ARTa, c/o Department of Speech Communication, Mount San Antonio College, Walnut, CA.

2. Have your instructor book an evening or two at a campus theatrical arena to present the best classroom examples of Readers Theatre before your quarter or semester is over.

3. Call a local elementary school, a service club, or an assisted-living home to see if they would be interested in having you perform a Readers Theatre presentation at a convenient time.

4. If you are connected to a religious organization, volunteer to compile a fitting RT-type program for a worship service, a youth group activity, or even a wedding. Find local members of the religious group to perform in your script.

5. If your instructor discovers a local festival or forensics tournament that offers a group performance of literature event, take advantage of the opportunity and go with your colleagues and participate.

Additional Reading

Adams, William. Chapter Eight, "Community" in *Institute Book of Readers Theatre: A Practical Guide for School, Theater, & Community*. Chapel Hill, NC: Professional Press, 2003.

Kleinau, Marion L., and McHughes, Janet Larsen. Chapter Ten, "Interpreters Theatre in Special Contexts," in *Theatres for Literature*. Sherman Oaks, CA: Alfred Publishing Company, Inc., 1980.

Ratliff, Gerald Lee. *Beginning Readers Theatre: A Primer for Classroom Performance*. Annandale, VA: ERIC Clearinghouse on Reading and Communication Skills, 1981.

References

1. Alan Wade, Ted Colson, William E. McDonnell and Isabel M. Crouch, "Interpretation Festivals in Colleges and Universities: Eastern, Southern, Central and Western States," in *Performance of Literature in Historical Perspectives*, edited by David W. Thompson (Lanham, MD: University Press of America, Inc., 1983), 359–391.

2. Personal interview. March 20, 2006.

3. Ibid.

4. Lillenas Publishing Company of Kansas City, Missouri, and Zondervan Publishing Company of Grand Rapids, Michigan, are two prominent publishing firms for religious readers theatre. See also in particular: Gordon C. Bennett, *Readers Theatre Comes to Church* (Colorado Springs, CO: Meriwether Publishing Ltd., 1985); Todd V. Lewis, *RT: A Readers Theatre Ministry* (Kansas City, MO: Lillenas Publishing Company, 1988); Todd V. Lewis, *RT Two: Two Scripts for Readers Theatre* (Kansas City, MO: Lillenas Publishing Company, 1990); Todd V. Lewis, RT for Christmas: Two Seasonal Readers Theatre Plays (Kansas City, MO: Lillenas Publishing Company, 1998).

Appendix

Dividing Lines in Poetry:
"The Changed Man"

Directions: Divide up the following lines to be read by either two or three people. Designate each reader as "1, 2, or 3." Use the designation "ALL" if you wish everyone to say the line chorally. List two numbers together if you wish two readers to read together (e.g., 12 or 23). Take 15 to 20 minutes to practice this reading and present it in front of your classmates:

"The Changed Man"
by Robert Phillips

If you were to hear me imitating Pavarotti in the shower every morning,

you would know how much you have changed my life.

If you were to see me stride across the park,

waving to a stranger,

then you would know I am a changed man—

like Scrooge

awakened from his bad dreams feeling feather-light,

angel-happy,

laughing the father of a long line of bright laughs—

"It is still not too late to change my life!"

It is changed.

Me, who felt short-changed.

Because of you I no longer hate my body.

Because of you I buy new clothes.

Because of you I'm a warrior of joy.

Because of you and me.

Drop by this Saturday morning and discover me

fiercely pulling weeds gladly, dedicated

as a born-again gardener.

Drop by on Sunday—I'll Turtlewax your sky-blue sports car, no sweat.

I'll greet enemies with a handshake,

forgive debtors

with a papal largesse.

It's all because of you.

Because of you and me,

I've become one changed man.

Dividing Lines for Drama Literature:
"The Glass Menagerie"

Directions: Use a pencil to divide the following dramatic script excerpt into lines for three or four performers, designated as 1, 2, 3, 4. Use subsequent numbering if you wish more than one performer to speak simultaneously. Say "ALL" for a complete choral reading.

Excerpt from "The Glass Menagerie"
by Tennessee Williams ©1945

Tom!

Yes, Mother?

Where are you all?

On the terrace, Mother.

Why don't you come in?

Mother, you look so pretty.

You know, that's the first compliment you ever paid me. I wish you'd look pleasant when you're about to say something pleasant, so I could expect it. Mr. O'Connor?

How do you do?

Well, well, well, so this is Mr. O'Connor? Introduction's entirely unnecessary. I've heard so much about you from my boy. I finally said to him, "Tom, good gracious, why don't you bring this paragon to supper finally? I'd like to meet this nice young man at the warehouse! Instead of just hearing you sing his praises so much?" I don't know why my son is so stand-offish—that's not Southern behavior. Let's sit down...

Mother, how about our supper?

Honey, you go ask sister if supper is ready! You know that sister is in full charge of supper. Tell her you hungry boys are waiting for it. [Tom exits through curtains and off left. Amanda turns to Jim.] Have you met Laura?

Well, she came to the door.

She let you in?

179

Yes, ma'am.

She's very pretty.

Oh, yes, ma'am…

Tom?

Yes, Mother.

What about that supper?...Where is Laura?

Laura is not feeling too well and thinks maybe she'd better not come to the table.

Laura!!!

Yes, Mother?

[motioning for Jim to be seated] Mr. O'Connor.

Thank you, ma'am.

Laura, we can't say grace till you come to the table.

[Laura enters, obviously quite faint, lips trembling, eyes wide and staring. Moves unsteadily toward dining room table.]

Oh, Mother, I'm so sorry. [Tom catches her as she faints]

Why, Laura, you are sick, darling! Laura—rest on the sofa. Well! [to Jim] Standing over the hot stove made her ill!—I told her that it was just too warm this evening, but—[to Tom] Is Laura all right now?

She's better, Mother.

My goodness, I suppose we're going to have a little rain! Tom, you say grace.

What?

What do we generally do before we have something to eat? We say grace, don't we?

For these and all Thy mercies—God's Holy Name be praised.

Dividing Performance Lines in Narrative Fiction: "The Final Problem"

Directions: Use a pencil to divide the following narrative fiction excerpt into lines for three or four performers, designated as 1, 2, 3, 4. Use subsequent numbering if you wish more than one performer to speak simultaneously. Say "ALL" for a complete choral reading.

"The Final Problem"
by Sir Arthur Conan Doyle

In a tingle of fear I was already running down the village street, and making for the path which I had so lately descended. It had taken me an hour to come down. For all my efforts, two more had passed before I found myself at the fall of Reichenbach once more. There was Holmes's alpenstock still leaning against the rock by which I had left him. But there was no sign of him, and it was in vain that I shouted. My only answer was my own voice reverberating in a rolling echo from the cliffs around me.

It was the sight of that alpenstock which turned me cold and sick....He had remained on that three-foot path, with sheer wall on one side and sheer drop upon the other, until his enemy had overtaken him....

I stood for a minute or two to collect myself, for I was dazed with the horror of the thing. Then I began to think of Holmes's own methods and to try to practice them in reading this tragedy. It was, alas! only too easy to do. During our conversation we had not gone to the end of the path, and the alpenstock marked the place where we had stood. The blackish soil is kept forever soft by the incessant drift of spray, and a bird would leave its tread upon it. Two lines of footmarks were clearly marked along the further end of the path, both leading away from me. There were none returning. A few yards from the end the soil was all ploughed up into a patch of mud, and the brambles and ferns which fringed the chasm were torn and bedraggled. I lay upon my face and peered over, with the spray spouting up all around me. It had darkened since I had left, and now I could only see here and there the glistening of moisture upon the black walls, and far away down at the end of the shaft the gleam of the broken water. I shouted; but only that same half-human cry of the fall was borne back to my ears.

But it was destined that I should after all have a last word of greeting from my friend and comrade. I have said that his alpenstock had been left leaning against a rock which jutted on to the path. From the top of this boulder the

181

gleam of something bright caught my eye, an, raising my hand, I found that it came from the silver cigarette case which he used to carry. As I took it up a small square of paper upon which it had lain fluttered down on to the ground. Unfolding it I found that it consisted of three pages torn from his notebook and addressed to me. It was characteristic of the man that the direction was as precise, and the writing as firm and clear, as though it had been written in his study.

"MY DEAR WATSON," he said, "I write these few lines through the courtesy of Mr. Moriarty, who awaits my convenience for the final discussion of those questions which lie between us. He has been giving me a sketch of the methods by which he avoided the English police and kept himself informed of our movements. They certainly confirm the very high opinion which I had formed of his abilities. I am pleased to think that I shall be able to free society from any further effects of his presence, though I fear that it is at a cost which will give pain to my friends, and especially, my dear Watson, to you. I have already explained to you, however, that my career had in any case reached its crisis, and that no possible conclusion to it could be more congenial to me than this. Indeed, if I may make a full confession to you, I was convinced that the letter from Meiringen was a hoax, and I allowed you to depart on that errand under the persuasion that some development of this sort would follow. Tell Inspector Patterson that the papers which he needs to convict the gang are in pigeonhole M, done up in a blue envelope and inscribed 'Moriarty.' I made every disposition of my property before leaving England, and handed it to my brother Mycroft. Pray give my greetings to Mrs. Watson, and believe me to be, my dear fellow,

"Very sincerely yours,
'SHERLOCK HOLMES.'"

A few words may suffice to tell the little that remains. An examination by experts leaves little doubt that a personal contest between the two men ended, as it could hardly fail to end in such a situation, in their reeling over, locked in each other's arms. Any attempt at recovering the bodies was absolutely hopeless, and there, deep down in that dreadful cauldron of swirling water and seething foam, will lie for all time the most dangerous criminal and the foremost champion of the law of their generation....As to the gang, it will be within the memory of the public how completely the evidence which Holmes had accumulated exposed their organisation, and how heavily the hand of the dead man weighed upon them. Of their terrible chief few details came out during the proceeding, and if I have now been compelled to make a clear statement of his career, it is due to those injudicious champions who have endeavoured to clear his memory by attacks upon him whom I shall ever regard as the best and wisest man whom I have ever known.

[Source: from Sir Arthur Conan Doyle, *The Memoirs of Sherlock Holmes* (©1893 A. Conan Doyle) New York: Harper & Brothers, 1894)]

Dividing Lines for Performances in Nonfiction Essays: "You Want Mind-Blowing?"

Directions: Use a pencil to divide the following narrative fiction excerpt into lines for three or four performers, designated as 1, 2, 3, 4. Use subsequent numbering if you wish more than one performer to speak simultaneously. Say "ALL" for a complete choral reading.

"You Want Mind-Blowing? Look at the Middle-Aged Brain"
by Dennis Palumbo

On the pages of medical journals and the cover of *Time* magazine, in feature stories on network news and nightly jokes in Jay Leno's monologue, there's been a swell of media coverage this past year concerning "the teenage brain."

Despite sounding like the title of Hollywood's latest horror-movie blockbuster, the phrase actually refers to recent neurological research on adolescent brain chemistry. It's finally been demonstrated empirically (to the surprise of practically no one not wearing a lab coat) that the teenage brain is different from that of a mature adult.

According to the data, these differences explain the average teen's inclination to stay up late, sleep until noon and exhibit extreme mood swings (for example, from sullen and defiant to *really* sullen and defiant). Some researchers have even blamed these brain differences for the adolescent's inexplicable devotion to high-decibel music, low-decibel mumbling and the piercing of unlikely body parts.

As soon as these results made national headlines, the usual social pundits—bored with Iraq, the Supreme Court nominee and Jessica Simpson's divorce—began hitting the TV talk-show circuit. This new research, they claimed, clearly suggested that we should ban teen driving and even raise the voting age. After all, we now had proof positive that today's teens are simply too erratic to be entrusted with such responsibilities.

This may be. But what about the *midlife* brain? Perhaps the next time we embark on exhaustive, heavily funded research into what's in the human skull, we should focus our efforts on the average middle-aged person—because if my friends and I are at all representative, I'd argue that whatever's going on in our collective brains is equally suspect.

Though not without good reason. Most adults I know are overworked, over-stressed and generally overwhelmed from their daily struggles with careers, child-rearing and relationships. They're forgetful, continually on a diet, obsessed with their health (popping pills to an extent no teenager would even contemplate), envious of their neighbors and co-workers, and always— always—sleep-deprived.

Frankly, even on a good day our brains are nothing to write home about. It's everything we can do to keep our complicated, must-have Starbucks coffee orders straight in our heads.

I think it's too easy to blame all this on brain chemistry. The truth is, life is hard, no matter how old you are. Whether you're worried about making the track team or paying the mortgage, about fitting in with the cool kids or impressing your new boss, it's about trying to cope.

Granted, your average teen's coping mechanisms may rarely extend beyond junk food and video games. But are adults' choices any better? Addicted to Internet porn, "Desperate Housewives," Tom Clancy novels and golf. Running from their yoga class to a Parents Without Partners meeting to the latest Donald Trump get-rich-quick seminar. And, between all this, compulsively checking e-mails and sending text messages on their cell phones (all the while nursing fantasies of winning the lottery, or running off to Tahiti with the office manager).

Let's face it, teens have just two basic goals: having sex and getting into a good college. Both are pretty laudable and straight-forward aims, especially when compared with the confusing and relentless demands of contemporary life with which grownups have to contend. It's no wonder that at the end of the day, most adults just want to collapse on the sofa and channel-surf.

Sartre once said that the state of modern man is incomprehension and rage. OK, maybe he was a bit of a Gloomy Gus. But isn't the bewilderment and struggle to which he alludes true at times for all of us, particularly at certain crucial stages in our life?

As a psychotherapist, I see daily the unfortunate consequences of assigning a diagnostic label to practically every kind of behavior under the sun. We need to remember that people are too complex to fit neatly into categories. Otherwise, we risk turning every character trait, coping mechanism and idiosyncrasy into a pathology. Let's not use these latest clinical data on adolescent brain chemistry, no matter how compelling, to do the same to teens—to reduce to a syndrome the myriad ways they struggle to cope with a very difficult developmental stage in a complex and often contra- dictory world.

And before we start debating whether teens should be allowed to drive and vote, we'd better be able to defend letting us adults do so. It's not as if our record in either of these endeavors is anything to brag about.

In other words, give the kids a break. They're not responsible for the way their brains develop, any more than they are for the world in which they have to grow up. The latter is the result of brains much older, and supposedly wiser, than theirs.

Transforming Single Persona to Multiple Personae in a Documentary

Directions: Choose three women to read the following excerpt from a documentary as if they are at times one persona and at other times more than one person, but ones who share the same experience. Designate readers as 1, 2, 3 and ALL if everyone speaks at the same time.

Excerpts from *The Prostitution Papers: A Candid Dialogue*
by Kate Millett

The way I got into it was like this. I was just broke and I never liked to be in debt to anyone…I just decided I'm not going to be poor any more.

I can never remember one job from another, but I do remember the first two. These days they all merge into a gray mass…Now, I never get sexually excited in any relationship with a john…Now I guess I'm sorta neuter. He never knows it, though, 'cuz I'm a great actress too.

This may sound funny coming from me, but prostitution not only puts down women, but it puts down sex—it really puts down sex. Often I really couldn't understand the customer, couldn't understand what he *got* outta this, because I really felt I was giving nothin'. What he got was nothin'… I felt sorry for him; the poor guy's gotta buy it—to have to offer somebody money…He's really gotta be hard up.

For me, the worst part about prostitution is that you're obliged not to sell sex only, but your humanity…what you're selling is your human dignity. Not really so much in bed, but in accepting the agreement—in becoming a bought person…It's selling your soul and not just selling a service….

I'm tellin' you—it's selling your own soul!

Excerpt from *The Prostitution Papers: A Candid Dialogue* by Kate Millett, 1973.

Group Activity on Generating "Creativity" in Readers Theatre

Directions: Jot down ideas on this page and act out with set pieces how you would demonstrate the following techniques for blocking, staging, and other creative performance choices.

The overall question for you to consider in this exercise is: **What techniques from other art forms are applicable to Readers Theatre?**

To get you started, below appears a list of general dramatizing problems in Readers Theatre:

Passage of Time
Transition of Place
Role Changes
Character Changes
Internalized States of Characters
Nonverbal Action
Physical Contact
Physical Setting

How could you use any of the following techniques from other art forms to adapt to Readers Theatre?

The Zoom Shot	The Tight Close-Up Shot
The Camera Cut	The Montage
Slow Motion	Speed Increases in Film
The Superimposed Image	The Camera Pan Shot
Sound-Mixing Overlay	The Dissolve
The Fade In/Fade Out Effect	Voice-Over Effect
Character Tags	Foreshadowing
Soliloquy	Aside
Confidant	Fourth Wall
Curtain or Wings	Thrust Stage
Movable Set	Landscape
Any others?????	

To think "creatively" you must:

1. Minimize set thinking.
2. Improvise alternatives for a solution when facing an obstacle.
3. Suspend critical judgment.
4. Provide opportunities to associate new concepts together.
5. Think like *MacGyver*.

AUDITION INFORMATION FOR:

_____

Name: _____

Telephone/Cell Number:_____

Address:_____

City:_____

E-mail Address: _____

Year in School:_____

Briefly summarize your RT or acting experience/list shows and years:

Rehearsals will be_____ nights from _____
beginning on _____; List any times you cannot make rehearsals:

You must be available during preview/dress rehearsal week for every session; you must be available to help load as well as take down the set (if necessary). Performances will be:

_____

AUDITION INFORMATION FOR:

_____

Name: _____

Telephone/Cell Number:_____

Address:_____

City:_____

E-mail Address: _____

Year in School:_____

Briefly summarize your RT or acting experience/list shows
and years:

Rehearsals will be _____ nights from _____
beginning on _____; List any times you cannot
make rehearsals:

You must be available during preview/dress rehearsal week for
every session; you must be available to help load as well as take
down the set (if necessary). Performances will be:

_____

PRODUCTION EVALUATION FORM

Evaluation of Director

Grade: _____

Name of the Director: _____

Title of the Readers Theatre Program: _____

Evaluating Commentary from Cast Member:

_____

_____

_____

_____

_____

_____

_____

_____

_____

_____

_____

_____

_____

PRODUCTION EVALUATION FORM

Evaluation of Director

Grade: _____

Name of the Director: _____

Title of the Readers Theatre Program: _____

Evaluating Commentary from Cast Member:

_____

_____

_____

_____

_____

_____

_____

_____

_____

_____

_____

_____

_____

PRODUCTION EVALUATION FORM

Evaluation of Participant (by the Director)

Grade: _____

Name of the Participant: _____

Evaluating Commentary from Director to the Cast Member:

_____

_____

_____

_____

_____

_____

_____

_____

_____

_____

_____

_____

_____

PRODUCTION EVALUATION FORM

Evaluation of Participant (by the Director)

Grade: _____

Name of the Participant: _____

Evaluating Commentary from Director to the Cast Member:

_____

_____

_____

_____

_____

_____

_____

_____

_____

_____

_____

_____

READERS THEATRE EVALUATION FORM

Title: _____

Readers:

1._____ 2._____ 3._____ 4._____

5._____ 6._____ 7._____ 8._____

PERFORMANCE COMMENTS:
Meaning of the Script Projected
Effective Pacing and Builds
Narration Effectiveness
Characterization
Projective Energy
Facial Reactions
Entrances/Exits
Focal Point Consistency
Promotion of Psychological Closure

STAGING VARIABLES:
Arrangement/Blocking
Movement and Timing
Choices for Clothing/Sets/
        Props/Music/Lighting
Creativity

SCRIPT EVALUATION COMMENTS:
Wholeness to Experience
Choice of Material
Clarity of Rhetorical Theme or Message
Logical Division of Lines
Variations between Group and Solo Aspects

GENERAL EFFECTIVENESS:
Projection of Intellectual Content
Projection of Emotional Content
Audience Responsiveness

Individual comments on performers found on the reverse side

READERS THEATRE EVALUATION FORM

Title: _____

Readers:

1._____ 2._____ 3._____ 4._____

5._____ 6._____ 7._____ 8._____

PERFORMANCE COMMENTS:
Meaning of the Script Projected
Effective Pacing and Builds
Narration Effectiveness
Characterization
Projective Energy
Facial Reactions
Entrances/Exits
Focal Point Consistency
Promotion of Psychological Closure

STAGING VARIABLES:
Arrangement/Blocking
Movement and Timing
Choices for Clothing/Sets/
        Props/Music/Lighting
Creativity

SCRIPT EVALUATION COMMENTS:
Wholeness to Experience
Choice of Material
Clarity of Rhetorical Theme or Message
Logical Division of Lines
Variations between Group and Solo Aspects

GENERAL EFFECTIVENESS:
Projection of Intellectual Content
Projection of Emotional Content
Audience Responsiveness

Individual comments on performers found on the reverse side

Index

Index

Index

Index

Index

Index